NorthStar

LISTENING AND SPEAKING
High Intermediate

SECOND EDITION

Tess Ferree
Kim Sanabria

Series Editors
Frances Boyd
Carol Numrich

Longman

NorthStar: Listening and Speaking, High Intermediate, Second Edition
Teacher's Manual and Achievement Tests

Pearson Education, 10 Bank Street, White Plains, NY 10606

Teacher's Manual by Barbara Sakamoto
Achievement Tests by Doray Espinosa and Jim Kahny

Test consultant: Tay Lesley

Development director: Penny Laporte
Project manager: Debbie Sistino
Senior development editor: Andrea Bryant
Vice president, director of design and production: Rhea Banker
Executive managing editor: Linda Moser
Production coordinator: Melissa Leyva
Senior production editor: Kathleen Silloway
Director of manufacturing: Patrice Fraccio
Senior manufacturing buyer: Dave Dickey
Cover design: Rhea Banker
Text design: Quorum Creative Services
Text composition: TSI Graphics
Text font: 11/13 Sabon

ISBN 0-201-78847-0

LONGMAN ON THE WEB

Longman.com offers online resources for
teachers and students. Access our Companion
Websites, our online catalog, and our local
offices around the world.

Visit us at **longman.com**.

Printed in the United States of America
7 8 9 10—TCS—09 08 07

Contents

Teacher's Manual

Achievement Tests

Introduction to the *NorthStar* Series

The *NorthStar* Approach to Language Teaching *NorthStar* is a five-level, integrated skills series for language learning. The series is divided into two strands: listening and speaking, and reading and writing. There are five books in each strand, taking students from the high beginning level of the *Introductory Student Book* to the advanced level of the *Advanced Student Book*. At each level, the two strands explore different aspects of the same contemporary themes. Each book practices language-learning skills through high-interest thematic content.

In addition to the Student Books, the *Writing Activity Book* for each level of the reading and writing strand expands and reinforces the writing process. The *Audio Program* includes, on CD or cassette, all the reading and listening segments as well as pronunciation exercises. The *Video Program* includes 3- to 5-minute segments for each unit. The segments are thematically linked to the units in the Student Books to offer additional material for listening comprehension and discussion or writing.

Integrated skills are at the heart of the *NorthStar* series. When two or more language skills are integrated, language learning is apt to be more authentic, natural, and motivating. Integrating skills offers more opportunity for recycling and reinforcing key vocabulary, grammatical structures, and ideas. As a result, students have more occasions to assimilate information and language, thereby facilitating learning.

Approach to Reading and Writing *NorthStar* supports the approach that learning to be a good writer means learning to be a good reader and vice versa. Reading skills are taught *implicitly* throughout each unit. For example, the comprehension exercises are designed to give practice in reading skills, such as predicting, identifying main ideas and details, skimming and scanning.

Writing skills are taught *implicitly* through the readings: The readings serve as models of good writing. In the Style section, writing skills are taught *explicitly* through analysis, explanation, and guided practice.

The writing process begins at the start of each unit (often with the first Prediction exercise), continues through the unit (with dialogues, written reactions to a partner's comments, chart completion, note taking), includes the Style section (with explicit writing skills and structured practice), and culminates in the Writing Topics section, where students are asked to produce a complete piece of writing.

Reading and writing skills—including strategies for improving vocabulary, comprehension, and grammar—are cultivated in every section of every unit. In the Research Topics section, the reading and writing integration becomes most clear and relevant, as students are asked to conduct research and read texts from a variety of authentic sources and then integrate ideas from these sources into their own writing.

Approach to Listening and Speaking *NorthStar* provides structured opportunities for students to practice listening to many types of discourse. Listening skills are taught *implicitly* throughout each unit. For example, the comprehension exercises are designed to give practice in such listening skills as predicting, identifying main ideas and details, and note taking.

Speaking skills are taught *implicitly* through the listenings: The listenings serve as models of functional language or conventional style. In the Style section, speaking skills are taught *explicitly* though analysis, explanation, a carefully structured pronunciation syllabus, and guided practice. The teaching of speaking begins at the start of each unit (often with the first Prediction exercise), continues through the unit (with categorizing and ranking activities, interviews, games, pronunciation practice, comparing answers and discussing differences, sharing opinions), includes the Style section (with explicit functional skills and structured practice), and culminates in the Speaking Topics section, where students use their speaking skills to create role plays, case studies, debates, radio announcements, and presentations.

Listening and speaking skills—including learning strategies for improving vocabulary, comprehension, and grammar—are cultivated in every section of every unit. In the Research Topics section, the listening and speaking integration becomes most clear and relevant as students are asked to conduct projects such as surveys or in-person and telephone interviews and then integrate ideas from these sources into their own oral presentations.

Approach to Grammar Content drives the organization of the grammar syllabus. Accordingly, students have opportunities to encounter and work with grammar structures in authentic contexts. The purpose of the Grammar section is to enable clear and accurate discussion and writing about the unit theme.

The Grammar section of each unit is not intended to be an exhaustive treatment of a grammatical point. Rather, it is an opportunity for students to focus on a new or familiar point within the specific context of the unit. Teachers and students can use the Grammar section either as the first step in presenting a particular structure or as a review. For more detailed explanations of the grammar points, a chart of Grammar Book References is included in the Student Books. This chart cross-references the unit grammar to appropriate sections in two successful grammar series: Azar's grammar series and *Focus on Grammar*.

Grammar is taught both inductively (through discovery) and deductively (through explanation). First, students answer questions to discover the form, usage, and meaning of the grammar. Next, they read an explanation of the point, with examples in the thematic context of the unit. Finally, students practice the structures in exercises related to the content of the unit.

Approach to Vocabulary Vocabulary practice has been increased in the Second Edition of *NorthStar*. Vocabulary is taught both *directly* and *indirectly*. Specific vocabulary exercises focus on meaning, usage, and word forms. In many of the other exercises (grammar, style, speaking and writing topics, research), the vocabulary reappears but is not the focus of the exercise.

In Section 1, Focus on the Topic, vocabulary has been chosen for its relevance in discussing the topic/theme. In other cases, the vocabulary is essential for comprehension of a listening or reading text, so the focus becomes preteaching vocabulary for comprehension. In Section 3, Focus on Vocabulary, the work takes on a different focus, as words are reviewed and studied in more depth. In this section, students are asked to go beyond the vocabulary presented in the text and explore new items. In the listening and speaking strand, a particular effort has been made to focus on idiomatic and informal expressions that are common in spoken English.

Correction in Oral Work
Students with academic and/or career goals need and want correction. You should listen to what students are saying on two levels: form and content. Use correction to help students close the gap between what they want to say and what they are able to say. Cued self-correction is preferable. Self-correction can be promoted in several ways. You will want to vary your strategies depending on the activity and time available.

- **On-the-spot correction:** As students are talking, you can use a nonverbal gesture (such as raising a finger, pulling an earlobe, writing the error on the board) to indicate that a correction is necessary.

- **Individual notes:** You may want to write down individual student's errors on a chart to have them corrected when the activity is finished. For example, in the Sample Error Chart below, general feedback is on the left-hand side. You can use symbols such as ↑ to mean "above average," → to mean "average," and ↓ to mean "below average." Specific feedback is on the right-hand side. An index card, divided into three equal parts, also works well.

Name *Maria R*	Class *English 101*	
General Feedback Fluency ↑ Accuracy → Pronunciation ↓	**Pronunciation/Stress** *these* /ð/ *think* /θ/	**Grammar/Vocabulary** *Yesterday, they say . . .* *The students works together . . .*
Notes *Interesting ideas about education.* *Be sure to speak loudly, too.* *Eye contact was much better.*	*rural* /r/ *official* *product*	*They have much problems . . .* *They needed a material subject.*

- **Collective notes:** You may want to take notes that can be used later to create an error-correction exercise.

- **Tapes and transcriptions:** You may want to use tapes and transcriptions to increase students' awareness of language errors. Audiotaping student conversations and reports is especially useful in the pronunciation activities in Sections 4A and 4D, where students have an opportunity for extensive oral production. First, tape the conversation, role play, or report; then record your feedback, modeling correct pronunciation. You can also transcribe a portion for use as an error-correction activity. Use blanks or underscoring to indicate errors; then have students correct their mistakes and encourage them to appreciate how their language is improving. Occasionally, it may be interesting to have students transcribe small bits of their own language for the same purpose.

If possible, you may want to videotape an activity. Play it back and elicit oral and written comments about students' own language and their feelings about seeing themselves speaking English. Follow this with some error correction on the board.

- **Fluency line:** Students need to develop fluency. The following activity develops fluency by giving students a chance to repeat the same story, explanation, or opinion to several different people.

  Divide the class in half. Have Group B students line up, side by side, and then have Group A students line up opposite them. Each Group A student then tells the Group B student opposite him or her a story, explanation, or opinion, depending on the assignment. Time the Group A students, giving them a set amount of time to talk. The Group A students must not stop talking, and the Group B students must not interrupt, except to ask for clarification. When you signal, all Group A students must take a step to the right and repeat their comments to their next Group B partner. (The Group A student at the end of the line has to walk around to the far left to find his or her new partner.) The activity continues with you signaling each partner to change. You can speed up the process by incrementally reducing the amount of time between partners. At a designated point, the roles are reversed so that Group B students have an opportunity to talk, and Group A students have an opportunity to listen.

  The format of this activity can be modified. For example, you could have students line up in concentric circles instead of lines or have them walk freely around the room, talking with different partners.

- **Audio journal:** An audio journal is like a written journal except that students record their ideas on an audio cassette tape instead of on paper. There are a number of assignments that can lead to audio journals—for example, comments on topics discussed in class, reports on individual research, and first drafts of oral presentations. Some teachers like to have students record pronunciation exercises as a way to individualize error correction. For all these activities, it is important to specify how long the students should speak and whether they should read prepared comments or speak extemporaneously. When you receive the audio journals, you can give students feedback by recording a reply right after their comments. When replying, be sure to discuss both content and form.

A Message from the Series Editors

We think of a good textbook as a musical score or a movie script. It tells you the moves and roughly how quickly and in what sequence to make them. But until you and your students bring it to life, a book is silent and static, a mere possibility. We hope that *NorthStar* orients, guides, and interests you as teachers.

It is our hope that the *NorthStar* series stimulates your students' thinking, which in turn stimulates their language learning, and that they will have many opportunities to reflect on the viewpoints of journalists, commentators, researchers, other students, and people in the community. Further, we hope that *NorthStar* guides them to develop their own point of view on the many and varied themes encompassed by this series.

We welcome your comments and questions. Please send them to us at the publisher:

Frances Boyd and Carol Numrich, Series Editors
NorthStar
Pearson Education
10 Bank Street
White Plains, NY 10606

Overview of the *Teacher's Manual and Achievement Tests*

The *NorthStar Teacher's Manual* includes:

- Specific suggestions for teaching each unit, including:
    - ✓ Unit-by-unit overview (scope and sequence) and summary
    - ✓ Unit-by-unit description of the Focus, Setup, and Expansion/Homework activities for each exercise
    - ✓ Suggested teaching times
    - ✓ Cross-references to the companion strand, Grammar Book References, *Writing Activity Book,* Video, and Companion Website

- The Answer Key to the Student Book

- Reproducible Achievement Tests with Answer Keys—including the test audioscript and test audio CD for the *Listening and Speaking* strand; and a test-generating CD-ROM to allow teachers to customize and adapt the 300 test items and writing tasks on the Reading and Writing Achievement Tests for the *Reading and Writing* strand

- An alphabetized-by-unit word list of the key vocabulary items practiced in each unit

---

COURSE PLANNER

Each unit contains approximately eight hours of classroom material, plus expansion, homework, and support material. Teachers can customize the units by assigning some exercises for homework and/or eliminating others. To help teachers customize the units for their specific teaching situation, the Unit-by-Unit Teaching Suggestions in the *Teacher's Manual* include 1, 2, or 3 stars to indicate the relative importance of each section or exercise:

        ✪✪✪ **Essential** sections
        ✪✪ **Recommended** sections
        ✪ **Optional** sections

To use *NorthStar* most effectively, see the teaching guide below.

CLASS TIME AVAILABLE PER UNIT	SECTIONS TO COMPLETE
8 hours or more	Essential (✪✪✪), Recommended (✪✪), Optional (✪)
6 hours	Essential (✪✪✪), Recommended (✪✪)
4 hours	Essential (✪✪✪) only

For News Resisters, No News Is Good News

OVERVIEW

Theme:	Media

Listenings:	Listening One: *News Resisters*
	    A radio news report
	Listening Two: *CornCam*
	    A report on an unusual Web site

Critical Thinking Skills:	Compare sources of news Recognize assumptions about media Interpret graphs Infer information not explicit in the interview Hypothesize another's point of view Analyze goals of news reporting
Listening Tasks:	Listen for main ideas Listen for details Provide evidence to support answers Relate listenings to personal values Synthesize information from both listenings Listen to student broadcasts and analyze them Evaluate a TV news program
Speaking Tasks:	Make predictions Summarize points Act out a scripted conversation Give a newscast Express and defend opinions Interview a news specialist
Pronunciation:	Reducing and contracting auxiliary verbs
Vocabulary:	Context clues Synonyms Idiomatic expressions Descriptive adjectives Dictionary work Word definitions
Grammar:	Passive voice

UNIT SUMMARY

This unit focuses on the positive and negative content of the news, and how the news influences individuals and society. Listening One is a radio interview with several news resisters. Listening Two is a radio interview with a man who created a website that shows corn growing.

The companion unit in *NorthStar: Reading and Writing* deals with the effects of tabloid journalism and the news media's intrusion into people's private lives.

1 Focus on the Topic, PAGE 1

✪✪✪ A   PREDICTING

Suggested Time: 10 minutes ⏱

Focus
To get students thinking about the role news plays in their lives; to predict the unit content from the title.

Setup
Have students work in pairs or small groups (of different language backgrounds or language levels, if possible) to look at the cartoon and discuss the questions. As a class, elicit answers to the questions from several of the students, trying to get a variety of opinions. For question 2, write a few of the suggested descriptions for "news resister" on the board to encourage discussion.

Expansion/Homework
You can also discuss these questions as a class without doing the pair work first. Try to elicit opinions from many students and encourage students to discuss ideas with each other.

✪✪ B   SHARING INFORMATION

Suggested Time: 20 minutes ⏱

Focus
To encourage free discussion of students' preferred sources of news.

Setup
Have students complete the survey individually before meeting in small groups. Ask students to compare their answers and discuss why some types of news media are better than others for certain types of information. Then have the students discuss their answers to Exercise 2. When they are done, ask the groups to report back to the class.

Expansion/Homework

To prepare for Exercise 2, you can ask your students to look back at the survey and write the approximate time they spend getting news from each source of news.

✪✪✪ C PREPARING TO LISTEN

BACKGROUND
Suggested Time: 20 minutes

Focus

To introduce the debate over the role of the news media in society; to explore Americans' opinions about news by looking at graphs.

Setup

Explain to students that they will be learning about the results of a national survey on people's opinions of the news. Have students read the introductory paragraph individually. Then put students in pairs (of similar fluency levels, if possible) to study the bar graphs. Student A reads the statements out loud, while Student B looks at the graphs and says whether the statements are true or false. Student B then corrects the false statements with information from the graphs. You can ask students to cover the half of the page that they are not supposed to look at. After the exercises are completed, ask students to react briefly to the information they learned, particularly if there are any survey results that surprise them.

Expansion/Homework

(1) You can also do this exercise as a guessing game. Have students cover the graphs on the right side of the page, and ask them to read the statements about Americans' opinions about the news and mark them **T** or **F**. Then have students look at the graphs and see if they guessed correctly. (2) To save time in class, the background paragraph can be read as homework and class time can be used to study the survey results.

VOCABULARY FOR COMPREHENSION
Suggested Time: 15 minutes

Focus

To introduce vocabulary and concepts related to news and the media to aid listening comprehension.

Setup

Have students pronounce the underlined words. Then pair them up (with a classmate sitting nearby) to read the sentences and circle the definitions of the underlined words—without using a dictionary. Have pairs take turns reading the exchanges, substituting the chosen definition for the underlined words (numbers 4 and 12 will require some adjusting to fit into the sentence). Go over the answers as a class.

Expansion/Homework

To save time, you can assign the definitions as homework and use class time to work on pronunciation and to check answers.

2 Focus on Listening, PAGE 8

✪✪✪ A | LISTENING ONE: *News Resisters*

Suggested Time: 10 minutes ⏲

Focus

To encourage students to make predictions about the benefits of reduced news intake; to become familiar with the speakers' voices.

Setup

Ask students to read the introductory paragraph and the prediction questions. Play the excerpt from the interview with Dr. Weil, and allow students time to compare their answers in pairs (of different fluency levels, if possible). Then elicit predictions from several students, affirming each prediction as a possibility.

Expansion/Homework

Have students write predictions, share them with a partner, and then discuss them with the class.

✪✪✪ LISTENING FOR MAIN IDEAS

Suggested Time: 15 minutes ⏲

Focus

To help students identify the main ideas of the radio interview.

Setup

Have students read through the multiple-choice questions. Play the interview once without stopping while students answer the questions. Have students compare their answers with those of a partner before going over them as a class.

✪✪✪ LISTENING FOR DETAILS

Suggested Time: 15 minutes ⏲

Focus

To get students to listen for specific details about the speaker's opinions.

Setup

Have students read the items and answer the questions they know. Play the report, and have students complete the exercise. If students seem to be having trouble, play the report one more time, and allow students to compare their answers with those of a partner. Go over the answers as a class. If disagreements arise, replay those segments rather than simply providing the answer.

✪✪ REACTING TO THE LISTENING
Suggested Time: 25 minutes ◉

Focus
To get students to infer opinions after listening to an interview, and to provide support for their inferences.

Setup
For Exercise 1, have students read the instructions. Then ask them to look at the questions for Excerpt One. Play Excerpt One and then stop the audio, allowing students time to write their answers. Replay the excerpt as needed so students can write down the language used by the speaker. Repeat this procedure for the other excerpts. During the discussions, make sure that students give reasons for their answers. Emphasize that it is possible for students to draw varying inferences, as long as their reasoning is sound. For Exercise 2, have students discuss the questions in small groups (of similar fluency levels, if possible).

Expansion/Homework
To teach students how to make inferences based on what they hear, you may want to do Excerpt One as a class. After playing the excerpt, elicit the students' answers to question 1. Then ask them to explain why they chose that answer. Write the information they provide as support on the board.

Link to *NorthStar: Reading and Writing*
If students are also using the companion text, you can ask them to speculate about how the interviewees would react to the "Peeping Tom Journalism" described in Reading One, pages 5–6.

✪✪✪ B LISTENING TWO: *CornCam*
Suggested Time: 20 minutes ◉

Focus
To introduce students to a Web site that shows corn growing in a field, and to encourage them to think about alternative views on what constitutes "news."

Setup
Read through the questions with the students. Play the radio interview, having students circle answers for the questions. Then play the interview again to allow students to check their answers. Replay the audio as needed. Next, have students select a reason for CornCam's popularity from the choices listed in Exercise 2. Replay the interview, instructing students to listen for information to support their choice. After listening, have students discuss their answers in pairs or as a class.

Expansion/Homework
Have students predict answers to questions before listening to the interview. After listening, have them adjust their answers based on the information from the interview.

Link to *NorthStar: Reading and Writing*

If students are using the companion text, you can have them skim the article about Richard Jewell on pages 9–10, and discuss how Dan Zinkat from *Iowa Farmer Today* would react to the way journalists covered the bombing story.

✪✪✪ C LINKING LISTENINGS ONE AND TWO

Suggested Time: 30 minutes

Focus

To get students to synthesize and react to the opinions they heard in Listenings One and Two, and to infer whether the news resisters from Listening One would like CornCam.

Setup

Ask students to think about the people they heard interviewed in Listening One and jot down notes. Then have students meet in groups (of differing language backgrounds or language levels, if possible). If needed, have students identify a key opinion for each person to help them remember interview responses. In groups, have students decide whether each person listed would like or dislike CornCam, and list reasons for their opinions. You may want to list the vocabulary from Vocabulary for Comprehension, pages 6–7, on the board to encourage students to use the vocabulary in their discussions. Then have the groups share some of their opinions with the class.

Link to *NorthStar: Reading and Writing*

If students are also using the companion text, you can list the vocabulary from Vocabulary for Comprehension, pages 6–7, on the board. Ask students to use the vocabulary in their discussion. For example, you can say: *Today there are many **tabloid** television news programs. Do you think the need for **networks** to find news around the clock makes ordinary people fair game for **journalists**?*

3 Focus on Vocabulary, PAGE 13

✪ EXERCISE 1
Suggested Time: 15 minutes

Focus

To reinforce and expand vocabulary studied in the unit; to have students practice using new vocabulary in the context of a paragraph.

Setup

Have students work individually or in small groups (of similar fluency levels, if possible) to match words and definitions. Encourage them to consult each other and their dictionaries before asking you for help. Check the answers as a class. Review the pronunciation of the words and have students practice repeating them. Then have students read the paragraph that follows, inserting the new words where appropriate. Check the answers as a class.

Expansion/Homework

You may want to assign the exercise as homework, and then use class time to check answers and correct pronunciation.

✪ EXERCISE 2
Suggested Time: 15 minutes ⏰

Focus

To determine whether words have positive, negative, or neutral connotations.

Setup

Model this exercise with a pair of words that are similar in meaning but have positive and negative connotations (e.g., *assertive/aggressive* or *determined/stubborn*). Have students work with partners and then compare answers as a class.

Expansion/Homework

You may want to assign the exercise as homework, and then use class time to check answers.

✪ EXERCISE 3
Suggested Time: 15 minutes ⏰

Focus

To have students use vocabulary presented in this unit in their own speaking.

Setup

Have students work in pairs asking and answering the questions, using the vocabulary given.

Expansion/Homework

You may want to ask several students to ask and answer the questions in front of the class, as an interview role play.

 For extra vocabulary practice, have students work on the self-grading vocabulary activities for the unit on the NorthStar Companion Website at **http://www.longman.com/northstar**.

4 Focus on Speaking, PAGE 16

✪✪ A PRONUNCIATION: Reducing and Contracting Auxiliary Verbs

Suggested Time: 15 minutes 🕐

Focus

To help students hear the reduced forms of *be* and *have* when they follow pronouns, and to practice using these reduced forms in conversation.

Setup

Read the example sentences in both unreduced and reduced forms. Help students to see that the reduced forms sound "friendlier" in conversation. Have students practice repeating the sentences using the reduced forms. For Exercise 1, have students listen to the sentences and underline the words that contain reduced sounds. Check answers as a class, and then have students practice reading the sentences with a partner. For Exercise 2, have students listen to the audio and fill in the missing words. Check answers as a class, and then have students practice reading the paragraph out loud with a partner.

Expansion/Homework

Have students predict which words will be reduced before listening, or predict (based on context and their knowledge of grammar) which words will go in the paragraph blanks.

✪✪ B GRAMMAR: Passive Voice

Suggested Time: 30 minutes 🕐

Focus

To have students practice using the passive voice, a grammatical point that will be used in the Speaking Topic, page 22, to discuss the news.

Setup

Discover students' existing knowledge by having them read the sentences and answer the questions in Exercise 1. Present the grammar, referring students to the grammar box on page 18. Then have students complete Exercise 2 individually. Check the answers by having each student write one answer on the board; then discuss any problems as a class. Put students in pairs (of different language levels, if possible) for Exercise 3. Check the answers by asking each pair to perform a line of dialogue while other students listen and correct the verb conjugations.

Expansion/Homework

(1) After checking Exercise 2, you can ask students to analyze why the passive voice was used in each case. Have them refer back to the three reasons in the grammar explanation on page 18. Discuss the reasons as a class. (2) For further practice, offer exercises from *Focus on Grammar, High Intermediate,* and *Understanding and Using English Grammar.* See the Grammar Book References on pages 231–232 of the Student Book for specific units and chapters.

❀❀❀ C | STYLE: Stating an Opinion

Suggested Time: 30 minutes

Focus

To help students practice stating opinions with varying degrees of strength, a language function that will be used in the Speaking Topic, page 22.

Setup

With books closed, ask students what they would say to express an opinion. Write the responses on the board. Ask what they would say to express a strong opinion and an opinion they are unsure about. Again, write the responses on the board. Then have students open their books and read the introductory explanation and list of expressions. Put students in small groups (of similar fluency levels, if possible), and ask them to take turns leading a discussion on each statement, soliciting responses from the other members of the group. Encourage students to expand on the discussions by explaining the reasons for their opinions.

Expansion/Homework

You can also do this activity as an opinion poll. Assign one question to each student. Have students move freely around the room, getting an answer from each of their classmates. Then have each student report on the class's answers, again using the expressions for stating an opinion (e.g., *Most people feel that . . .* or *Two people are not sure . . .* or *One person feels strongly that . . .*).

Link to *NorthStar: Reading and Writing*

If students are also using the companion text, you can also have them examine the paragraphs in Exercise 2, pages 19–20. Have students identify the opinions expressed in each paragraph, and decide how strongly each opinion is stated.

 For extra listening practice, use the NorthStar Companion Video.

❀❀❀ D | SPEAKING TOPIC

Suggested Time: 50 minutes

Focus

To give students a chance to use the knowledge, vocabulary, and skills they have learned in the unit to think about what types of news programming might attract news resisters.

Setup

Assign students to groups of three to four. To get students started, discuss the suggested objectives for their television broadcast. Then let students work in their groups, giving them a time limit (about 15 minutes) to read the summaries in Step 2 and decide how to present them to reflect one of the objectives. Have students move on to Step 3, remaining in the same groups. Read through the directions with the class. Remind students to use the passive voice in their news broadcast. Finally, have the groups present their broadcast to the class.

Expansion/Homework

(1) To help students get ideas about the use of passive voice in news broadcasts, either replay Listening One or Two, or bring in examples of actual news stories on video. (2) To help students give each other feedback after the presentations in Step 4, you can have students take notes on the approach or angle chosen by each group. Then, after each presentation, the groups can meet to quickly evaluate the approaches. Ask them to evaluate their broadcasts in terms of whether the news resisters interviewed in Listening One would be attracted to the stories as presented. For those stories that they decide would not appeal, have them make suggestions for improvement.

⊕E RESEARCH TOPICS

Activity 1: Analyzing a News Program
Suggested Time: 30 minutes ⊚

Focus
To apply the concepts of purpose to real news broadcasts.

Setup
Make sure your students have access to a television or radio. If possible, devise a list of possible news programs they can watch or listen to (including the station and time), and assign a different program to each student or group of students. Go over the assignment, and make sure that students understand the various goals listed on the chart. You may want to suggest that they take notes on a separate piece of paper while they listen to the news and transfer information to the chart later. After completing the listening task, have the students present their results to the class or in small groups. You can ask each student to describe the first five stories that appeared in the news show, saying whether they thought the stories met any of the goals listed. After two or three presentations, ask the class to compare the news programs and discuss what type of news they contain and why they differ.

Expansion/Homework
(1) You may want to list the words from Focus on Vocabulary, pages 13–16, on the board to encourage students to use the words during the discussion. (2) To give students feedback on this project, you can ask them to hand in a copy of the completed chart and write a brief analysis of the program, using the words from Focus on Vocabulary. They can discuss which news goals the program accomplished, or who is the audience for this news. You can evaluate students for their listening comprehension and their ability to use the concepts from the unit in their analyses.

Link to *NorthStar: Reading and Writing*
If students are also using the companion text, you can ask them to analyze whether the news show they watched contained sensational, tabloid-style reporting. If so, ask them to give some examples of the sensational style of coverage.

Activity 2: Visiting a Local Newspaper, TV Station, or Radio Station
Suggested Time: 30 minutes 🕐

Focus

To learn more about newspaper, TV, and radio issues presented in the unit.

Setup

Arrange for students to visit a local newspaper, TV station, or radio station; or invite an editor, publisher, or reporter to speak in your class. Before the visit, help students prepare a list of questions to ask. You may want students to brainstorm questions on the different topics in small groups and then come together as a class to prepare a final list. Under the category of "content," you can help students develop some questions about the coverage of "good news" versus "bad news." Assign one or two questions to each student. After the visit, have students meet in groups to prepare a summary of what they learned.

Link to *NorthStar: Reading and Writing*

If students are also using the companion text, you can help them develop some questions about the use of tabloid-style reporting.

The Achilles Heel

OVERVIEW

Theme:	Overcoming Obstacles

Listenings:	Listening One: *Dreams of Flying and Overcoming Obstacles*
	    A college application essay
	Listening Two: *The Achilles Track Club Climbs Mount Kilimanjaro*
	    A television news report

Critical Thinking Skills:	Identify personal obstacles Rank the value of personal qualities Analyze narrative techniques in an essay Hypothesize another's point of view Analyze sensitive language referring to disabilities Infer meaning not explicit in the text Compare and contrast two life histories Frame contrasting points of view on disability issues
Listening Tasks:	Summarize main ideas Listen for details Relate listening to knowledge of the world Identify connecting themes between two listenings Identify thought groups in speech Watch and analyze a movie Listen to classmates' reports and pose questions
Speaking Tasks:	Make predictions Construct and perform a dialogue Practice using synonyms, parallelism, and prepositional phrases to enrich a narrative Plan and give a three-minute speech Orally summarize research on overcoming obstacles
Pronunciation:	Thought groups
Vocabulary:	Context clues Word definitions Figurative language
Grammar:	Gerunds and infinitives

UNIT SUMMARY

This unit focuses on people with disabilities and how they have overcome obstacles in their lives. Listening One is a radio broadcast of a student's college application essay. Listening Two is a news broadcast focusing on a group of disabled athletes who climbed Mount Kilimanjaro.

The companion unit in *NorthStar: Reading and Writing* deals with people who have overcome adversity in their lives.

1 Focus on the Topic, PAGE 25

✪✪✪A PREDICTING

Suggested Time: 10 minutes ⏱

Focus
To get students thinking about the sorts of obstacles people might have to overcome; to predict the unit content from the title.

Setup
Have students work in pairs or small groups (of different language backgrounds or language levels, if possible) to look at the photograph and discuss the questions. As a class, elicit answers to the questions from several of the students, trying to get a variety of opinions. For question 1, write a few of the suggested obstacles on the board to encourage brainstorming.

Expansion/Homework
You can also discuss these questions as a class without doing the pair work first. Try to elicit opinions from many students and encourage students to discuss ideas with each other.

✪✪B SHARING INFORMATION

Suggested Time: 20 minutes ⏱

Focus
To encourage free discussion of students' personal experience with life obstacles.

Setup
Go over the list of obstacles as a class, explaining terms that may be unfamiliar. Elicit examples of each type of obstacle, if desired. Have students select one of the obstacles from the list. Then with a partner or in a small group, have them discuss their (or another person's) experience with that obstacle, using the questions to guide discussion. When they are done, ask the groups to report back to the class.

Expansion/Homework

If students feel uncomfortable discussing personal experiences, instruct them to select a well-known person (such as a celebrity, athlete, politician, or leader) and discuss that person's experience overcoming obstacles.

✪✪✪ C   PREPARING TO LISTEN

BACKGROUND
Suggested Time: 20 minutes

Focus
To introduce the American value of overcoming obstacles; to give students background information about college admissions essays.

Setup
Have students read the introductory paragraph individually. Then put students in pairs (of similar fluency levels, if possible) to study the list of personal qualities. Working together, have them add two more qualities to the list, and then pick the top three qualities they believe would be most important. After the exercise is completed, ask students to share the qualities they added and selected as being most important.

Expansion/Homework
To save time in class, the background paragraph can be read as homework, and class time can be used to discuss the list of qualities.

VOCABULARY FOR COMPREHENSION
Suggested Time: 15 minutes

Focus
To introduce vocabulary and concepts related to obstacles and overcoming them.

Setup
Have students pronounce the boldfaced words. Then pair students up (with a classmate sitting nearby) to read the sentences, and have them insert the correct choice from the vocabulary list. Go over the answers as a class.

Expansion/Homework
To save time, you can assign the definitions as homework and use class time to work on pronunciation and check answers.

✷ Focus on Listening, PAGE 28

✪✪✪ A ▐ LISTENING ONE: *Dreams of Flying and Overcoming Obstacles*

Suggested Time: 10 minutes ⏱

Focus

To encourage students to make predictions about how one college application essay might be special; to become familiar with the speakers' voices.

Setup

Ask students to read the introductory paragraph and the prediction questions. Play the excerpt from the interview with Bob Edwards, and allow students time to compare their answers in pairs (of different fluency levels, if possible). Then elicit predictions from several students, affirming each prediction as a possibility.

Expansion/Homework

Have students write predictions, share them with a partner, and then discuss them with the class.

✪✪✪ LISTENING FOR MAIN IDEAS

Suggested Time: 15 minutes ⏱

Focus

To help students identify the main ideas of the radio interview.

Setup

Have students read through the questions. Play the interview once without stopping while students answer the questions. Have students compare their answers with those of a partner before checking them with the class.

✪✪✪ LISTENING FOR DETAILS

Suggested Time: 15 minutes ⏱

Focus

To get students to listen for specific details in Richard Van Ornum's college application essay.

Setup

Have students read the items and answer the questions they know. Then play the report, and have students complete the exercise. If students seem to be having trouble, play the report one more time and allow students to compare their answers with those of a partner. Go over the answers as a class. If disagreements arise, replay those segments rather than simply providing the answer.

✪✪ REACTING TO THE LISTENING
Suggested Time: 25 minutes 🕘

Focus
To get students to link related words and phrases; to evaluate Richard's experience.

Setup
For Exercise 1, have students read the instructions. Then ask them to look at the questions for Excerpt One. Play Excerpt One and then stop the audio, allowing students time to write their answers. Replay the excerpt as needed so students can write down the language used by the speaker. Repeat this procedure for the other excerpts. During the discussions, make sure that students give reasons for their answers. Emphasize that it is possible for students to answer the questions in different ways, as long as their reasoning is sound. For Exercise 2, have students discuss the questions in small groups (of similar fluency levels, if possible).

Expansion/Homework
Have students answer the discussion questions individually, before starting discussion.

Link to *NorthStar: Reading and Writing*
If students are also using the companion text, you can ask them to read Reading One on pages 26–29 and speculate what experiences Frank McCourt might have chosen to highlight in his college application essay.

✪✪✪ B LISTENING TWO: *The Achilles Track Club Climbs Mount Kilimanjaro*
Suggested Time: 20 minutes 🕘

Focus
To introduce students to a group of disabled athletes who climbed Mount Kilimanjaro; to encourage them to think about the different terms used to describe people with disabilities.

Setup
Read through the questions with the students. Play the interview and have students answer the questions in Exercise 1. Then play the interview again to allow students to check their answers. Replay the audio as needed. Next, have students work in pairs for Exercises 2 and 3. Discuss their answers as a class.

Expansion/Homework
Introduce additional terms for referring to people who are blind (e.g., visually impaired) and deaf (e.g., hearing impaired), and discuss feelings people might associate with the different terms.

Link to *NorthStar: Reading and Writing*
If students are using the companion text, you can have them skim the article by Diane Schuur on pages 32–33, and discuss what term Diane might prefer to use to describe herself (rather than "handicapped").

✪✪✪ C | **LINKING LISTENINGS ONE AND TWO**

Suggested Time: 30 minutes ⏱

Focus
To get students to compare and contrast the experiences of Richard Van Ornum and the Achilles Track Club in Listenings One and Two.

Setup
Go over the questions as a class, and ask students to complete the chart. In pairs, have students compare their answers, and then discuss them as a class. You may want to list on the board the vocabulary from Sharing Information, page 26, to encourage students to use the vocabulary in their discussions. Then have the groups share some of their opinions with the class.

Link to *NorthStar: Reading and Writing*
If students are also using the companion text, have them add information to this chart for Frank McCourt and Diane Schuur, and compare their challenges to those of Richard Van Ornum and the Achilles Track Club.

❸ Focus on Vocabulary, PAGE 33

✪ EXERCISE 1
Suggested Time: 15 minutes ⏱

Focus
To reinforce and expand vocabulary studied in the unit; to have students practice using new vocabulary in the context of journal entries.

Setup
Have students work individually or in small groups (of similar fluency levels, if possible) to use the listed vocabulary words to complete each journal entry. Encourage them to consult each other and their dictionaries before asking for your help. Check the answers as a class. Review the pronunciation of the words, and have students practice repeating them. Then have students take turns reading the completed entries.

Expansion/Homework
You may want to assign the exercise as homework, and then use class time to check answers and correct pronunciation.

✪ EXERCISE 2
Suggested Time: 15 minutes ⏱

Focus
To understand the difference between literal and figurative meanings of words.

Setup

Look at the example together, and if possible elicit additional examples of words or phrases students know that have both literal and figurative meanings. Then have students work with partners to identify the literal and figurative use of words in the sentences. Compare answers as a class.

Expansion/Homework

You may want to assign the exercise as homework, and then use class time to check answers.

✪ EXERCISE 3

Suggested Time: 15 minutes ⏱

Focus

To have students use vocabulary presented in this unit in their own speaking.

Setup

Go over the underlined words as a class. Then have students work in pairs, taking turns asking and answering the questions, using the underlined vocabulary in their answers.

Expansion/Homework

You may want to ask several students to ask and answer the questions in front of the class, as an interview role play.

 For extra vocabulary practice, have students work on the self-grading vocabulary activities for the unit on the NorthStar Companion Website at **http://www.longman.com/northstar**.

4 Focus on Speaking, PAGE 36

✪✪ A PRONUNCIATION: Thought Groups

Suggested Time: 15 minutes ⏱

Focus

To help students use thought groups to improve their speaking fluency.

Setup

Read the explanation and examples of thought groups in the box. Help students see that speaking in thought groups makes conversation sound more natural. Have students practice repeating the sentences, pausing between thought groups. In Exercise 1, have students listen to the sentences and underline the thought groups. Check answers as a class, and then have students practice reading the sentences with a partner. For Exercise 2, have students read the first thought group in column 1. Then have them complete the sentence by selecting appropriate thought groups from columns 2, 3, and 4. Check answers as a class, and then have students practice reading the sentences out loud to a partner. For Exercise 3, have students work on creating a conversation in pairs.

Expansion/Homework
Have students write each completed sentence from Exercise 2 on a separate sheet of paper (or on the board) and have them try to read them without pausing between thought groups. (Once they've learned how thought groups work, they should find this difficult.) Then read the sentences with the correct pauses, and compare how the thought groups aid comprehension. For Exercise 3, have students perform their conversations for the class as a role play.

✪✪ B GRAMMAR: Gerunds and Infinitives

Suggested Time: 30 minutes

Focus
To have students practice using gerunds and infinitives, a grammatical point that appeared in the listenings, and will be used in the Speaking Topics, page 43, in student speeches.

Setup
Discover students' existing knowledge by having them work in pairs to read the sentences and answer the questions in Exercise 1. Present the grammar, referring students to the grammar box on page 39. Then have students complete Exercise 2 with a partner. Check the answers by having each student write one answer on the board; then discuss any problems as a class. Have students work with a partner to complete the chart for Exercise 3. Compare answers as a class.

Expansion/Homework
(1) To save time, you can have students complete the chart as homework and use class time to discuss their answers. (2) For further practice, offer exercises from *Focus on Grammar, High Intermediate,* and *Understanding and Using English Grammar.* See the Grammar Book References on pages 231–232 of the Student Book for specific units and chapters.

✪✪✪ C STYLE: Using Narrative Techniques

Suggested Time: 30 minutes

Focus
To help students practice using synonyms, parallelism, and prepositional phrases of location to make their speech more vivid—techniques that will be used in the Speaking Topics, page 43.

Setup

Have students read the introductory explanations and examples of narrative techniques. For Exercise 1, put students in pairs (of similar fluency levels, if possible), and ask them to read the newspaper clipping and mark uses of synonyms or closely related words, parallelism, and prepositional phrases about physical location. Encourage students to discuss their choices. Then, in Exercise 2, have pairs use the narrative techniques they've identified to change the point of view in the clipping to that of one of the members of the Achilles Track Club.

Expansion/Homework

Have students change the clipping to reflect a different challenge the Achilles Track Club might have attempted (e.g., sailing across the Pacific, surviving on an island).

Link to *NorthStar: Reading and Writing*

If students are also using the companion text, you can also have them examine the paragraph about Greg Barton, page 40. Have students identify the narrative techniques used by the writer, and decide if the paragraph might be made more vivid by increased use of the narrative techniques studied.

 For extra listening practice, use the NorthStar Companion Video.

✪✪✪ D   SPEAKING TOPICS

Suggested Time: 50 minutes 🕐

Focus

To give students a chance to use the knowledge, vocabulary, and skills they have learned in the unit to present a two-to-three minute speech about an important time in their lives or an obstacle they have overcome; to have students present an oral version of a college application essay.

Setup

For Exercise 1, have students use the chart on page 43 to brainstorm and then plan their speeches. If desired, have students talk through their ideas with a partner and then practice their speeches with a partner before presenting for the entire class. For Exercise 2, have students work in small groups (of mixed fluency levels, if possible). Students should brainstorm their ideas for a college application essay and then work on an oral version of their essay individually. Have students present their oral essays to the class and then return to their groups to discuss what each person's presentations revealed about his or her personalities, and whether the presentations would work well as written essays. Encourage students to support their opinions.

Expansion/Homework

For Exercise 1, videotape student speeches to show to other classes or to use in evaluating students' nonverbal communication as they speak. For Exercise 2, have students turn their oral presentations into written essays. Collect the essays, copy them, and have students put together personal albums about the challenges they and their classmates have faced and overcome.

⭐E RESEARCH TOPICS

Activity 1: Evaluating a Movie
Suggested Time: 30 minutes 🕐

Focus
To explore how movies portray the heroism and achievements of people who have overcome obstacles.

Setup
Make sure your students have access to a television and VCR or DVD player. If possible, create a list of possible movies to start students in their research, and assign students to groups. If students will be watching the movie outside of class, be sure they are physically able to meet to watch the movie. After students watch their movie, have the groups report back to the class, describing the movie and how it shows someone overcoming obstacles.

Expansion/Homework
You may want to have students work on their research in groups and then present their recommendation to the class for discussion. As a class, have students select one movie and watch it together in class.

Link to *NorthStar: Reading and Writing*
If students are also using the companion text, you can ask them to see if they can find movies featuring the people listed on page 45 and the obstacles the people overcame.

Activity 2: Visiting a Library
Suggested Time: 30 minutes 🕐

Focus
To learn more about coverage of disabilities in magazine and newspaper articles.

Setup
Arrange for students to visit a local or campus library. If possible, ask to have a librarian demonstrate how to conduct a topic search of magazine and newspaper articles. Before the visit, help students prepare a list of possible topics to research. You may want students to brainstorm ideas on the different topics in small groups and then come together as a class to prepare a final list. Assign one or two topics to each student. After the visit, have students meet in groups to prepare a summary of what they found.

Link to *NorthStar: Reading and Writing*
If students are also using the companion text, have them perform a similar search for magazine and newspaper articles about the people listed on page 45.

Early to Bed, Early to Rise . . .

OVERVIEW

Theme:	Medicine
Listenings:	Listening One: *Teen Sleep Needs* A radio news report Listening Two: *Get Back In Bed* A conversation with a doctor
Critical Thinking Skills:	Interpret a cartoon Interpret a quotation Compare and contrast sleep habits Hypothesize scenarios Draw conclusions about sleep deprivation Propose solutions to problems Analyze a case of sleep deprivation and its consequences
Listening Tasks:	Converse with a classmate and take notes Summarize main ideas Listen for details Interpret speaker's tone and emotions Relate listening to personal experiences Compare information from two listenings Identify emphasis in speech and its meaning
Speaking Tasks:	Make predictions Use new vocabulary in a guided conversation Make contrastive statements using appropriate intonation Act out scripted dialogues Interrupt politely to clarify or confirm information Role-play a meeting Conduct a survey and report results
Pronunciation:	Contrastive stress
Vocabulary:	Context clues Word definitions
Grammar:	Present unreal conditionals

UNIT SUMMARY

This unit focuses on sleep habits and sleep deprivation. Listening One is a radio interview with experts regarding teenagers' sleep needs. Listening Two is an interview with a busy mother who is sleep deprived.

The companion unit of *NorthStar: Reading and Writing* deals with nonmedical ways of curing illness, including prayer and "laugh therapy."

1 Focus on the Topic, PAGE 45

✪✪✪A PREDICTING

Suggested Time: 10 minutes 🕐

Focus
To get students to predict the unit content from a cartoon; to discuss why people believe that adequate sleep is important.

Setup
Have students work in pairs (of different language backgrounds or language levels, if possible) to look at the cartoon and discuss the questions. Then, as a class, elicit answers to the questions from several of the students, trying to get a variety of responses.

Expansion/Homework
You can also ask students to look at the cartoon and predict what will happen next.

✪✪B SHARING INFORMATION

Suggested Time: 20 minutes 🕐

Focus
To encourage discussion of students' personal sleep habits.

Setup
Have students work in pairs. Have students take turns asking each other the questions in the chart and completing the chart with their answers. Then, as a class, have pairs report their findings.

Expansion/Homework
(1) Compile student responses in a class chart of sleep habits. (2) You can have students complete the chart with their own information (as homework or in class) before putting them in pairs.

✪✪✪C PREPARING TO LISTEN

BACKGROUND
Suggested Time: 20 minutes ⏱

Focus
To familiarize students with American sleep habits; to predict the results of sleep research studies.

Setup
Have students read the introduction individually and match categories with percentages. Then have students compare their answers with those of other students, discussing reasons for their answers.

Expansion/Homework
(1) You can have students assign percentages to each category in pairs or small groups. (2) To save time, you can assign the introduction and matching exercise as homework, using class time for comparison and discussion.

VOCABULARY FOR COMPREHENSION
Suggested Time: 20 minutes ⏱

Focus
To introduce vocabulary and concepts related to sleep and sleep deprivation; to aid listening comprehension.

Setup
Read out loud the e-mail and response as students follow along. Then have students work individually to match each underlined word with the appropriate synonym. Go over the answers as a class.

Expansion/Homework
You can assign the exercise as homework and use class time to work on pronunciation and check answers.

2 Focus on Listening, PAGE 50

✪✪✪A LISTENING ONE: *Teen Sleep Needs*
Suggested Time: 10 minutes ⏱

Focus
To encourage students to make predictions about teenagers' sleep needs.

Setup

Ask students to read the introductory paragraph and the prediction questions. Then play the excerpt from the radio interview. Have students answer the questions, then play the excerpt again and ask students to predict the answer to question 4, sharing their answers in pairs (of different fluency levels, if possible). Elicit predictions from several students. Affirm each prediction as a possibility.

✪✪✪ LISTENING FOR MAIN IDEAS
Suggested Time: 15 minutes ⏱

Focus

To help students identify the main ideas expressed in the interview.

Setup

Have students read the items and predict the answers they might hear. Play the report, and have students answer the questions. Pause the interview to allow adequate time for writing answers. If students seem to have trouble, play the audio one more time. Go over the answers. If disagreements arise, replay those segments rather than simply giving the answer. Then have students look back at the predictions they made in Listening One, page 50, to see how close they were.

✪✪✪ LISTENING FOR DETAILS
Suggested Time: 15 minutes ⏱

Focus

To get students to listen for specific details from the interview.

Setup

Have students read the questions and possible answers and answer those that they can. Then have students listen to the interview and circle the correct answers. Play the audio once more for students to check their answers.

✪✪ REACTING TO THE LISTENING
Suggested Time: 20 minutes ⏱

Focus

To get students to make inferences about the speakers' feelings based on tone of voice and word choice.

Setup

For Exercise 1, have students read the questions for Excerpt One. Play the excerpt, and then allow students to discuss their answers with a partner, refining their responses. Emphasize that it's possible for students to have varying opinions as long as their reasoning is sound. Replay the excerpt as needed while the pairs are discussing it. Then ask the pairs to share their answers with the class. Repeat the procedure for Excerpts Two, Three, and Four. For Exercise 2, have student pairs (of similar speaking abilities, if possible) discuss the three questions.

Expansion/Homework

(1) To teach students how to analyze the excerpts, you may want to do Excerpt One as a class. After playing the excerpt, elicit students' answers and write them on the board, asking for specific examples to illustrate the students' opinions. (2) Encourage students to draw comparisons from their own experiences as students.

✪✪✪ B   LISTENING TWO: *Get Back in Bed*

Suggested Time: 25 minutes

Focus

To explore the negative results of sleep deprivation and to realize how common the problem is.

Setup

Have students look at the questions, and predict their answers. Play Listening Two, and then have students circle their answers for questions 1–7. Play the interview again to allow students to check their answers.

Expansion/Homework

In pairs, have students compare their own experiences with those of the people mentioned in the interview.

✪✪✪ C   LINKING LISTENINGS ONE AND TWO

Suggested Time: 30 minutes

Focus

To get students to synthesize the information they have heard in Listenings One and Two, and to apply what they have learned to their own situations.

Setup

Read through the directions for the exercise with the students. Have students work in small groups (of similar fluency levels, if possible) to complete the chart with information from Listenings One and Two. Replay sections of the listenings, if requested. Then have students (in the same groups) answer the questions below the chart. Encourage students in the groups to help each other expand on their answers by asking leading questions. The groups can briefly report back to the class after their discussions.

Expansion/Homework

You can ask students to summarize their group's experience with sleep and sleep deprivation and report back to the class. Have students look for the similarities and differences in their experiences.

Link to *NorthStar: Reading and Writing*

If students are also using the companion text, you can ask them to skim Reading Two, page 56, and imagine that Norman Cousins is a guest on the *Satellite Sisters* radio show. What sorts of questions do you think the sisters would ask? Would they support his approach to treatment? Why?

❸ Focus on Vocabulary, PAGE 56

✪ EXERCISE 1
Suggested Time: 15 minutes ⏱

Focus
To reinforce and expand upon the new vocabulary in this unit.

Setup
Read the underlined vocabulary words aloud. Encourage students to repeat the words for pronunciation practice. Then have students read the passages and match the underlined words with the synonyms that follow.

Expansion/Homework
You can assign the exercise as homework and use class time to work on pronunciation and check answers.

✪ EXERCISE 2
Suggested Time: 15 minutes ⏱

Focus
To have students talk about their sleep habits in a question-and-answer format.

Setup
Have students work in pairs. Student A asks question 1; Student B (who has the questions covered) answers the question using the vocabulary items listed; then Student A makes an additional comment on Student B's answer. Have students switch roles after question 3.

Expansion/Homework
Have students who finish quickly think of additional questions to ask each other. Direct them to the vocabulary on page 56, and encourage them to use the new vocabulary in their answers.

 For extra vocabulary practice, have students work on the self-grading vocabulary activities for the unit on the NorthStar Companion Website at **http://www.longman.com/northstar**.

❹ Focus on Speaking, PAGE 58

✪✪ A   PRONUNCIATION: Contrastive Stress
Suggested Time: 30 minutes ⏱

Focus
To help students learn to use stress and pitch to emphasize and contrast words.

Setup

Read the explanation together. Have students repeat the example sentences, exaggerating the stress and pitch patterns. For Exercise 1, have students listen to the recorded sentences and underline the contrasted words. Then have students take turns reading the sentences with a partner. For Exercise 2, have students take turns asking and answering the questions in the sleep quiz. Have them report their findings to the class, using contrastive stress to compare their answers. In Exercise 3, go over the information in the chart as a class. Then, in pairs, have students make sentences using contrastive stress to compare the information from the chart. Go over answers as a class. For Exercise 4, do the model questions and answers together to give students a chance to practice reading them with different contrastive stresses to emphasize different information. Then have students work in pairs on the remaining questions and answers.

Expansion/Homework

Have students come up with original questions for Exercises 2 and 4.

Link to *NorthStar: Reading and Writing*

If students are also using the companion text, you can give them more practice using contrastive stress to communicate meaning by asking them to choose one paragraph from Reading One, "Dying for Their Beliefs," pages 51–53. Ask them to read the paragraph aloud three times—one time using stress to show that they support the parents' choice, one time as a neutral reporter, and one time using stress to show they disagree with the parents' choice.

✪✪B GRAMMAR: Present Unreal Conditionals

Suggested Time: 50 minutes 🕑

Focus

To have students practice using present unreal conditionals, a grammatical point that will be used in the Speaking Topic, page 65, to discuss sleep problems.

Setup

Discover students' existing knowledge by having them answer the questions in Exercise 1. Present the grammar point, referring students to the grammar box on pages 60–61. Then have students work individually to complete the sentences in Exercise 2. When they are finished, have them take turns reading the conversations expressively with a partner. For Exercise 3, have students work in small groups (of different language backgrounds, if possible) to practice asking for and giving advice about sleep problems. Remind students to use vocabulary from the unit and unreal conditionals from the grammar box and Exercise 2. Monitor the discussions, making grammatical and other corrections as necessary.

...ion/Homework

...heck the students' grammar individually, you can ask them to write short
...es to one of the problems in Exercise 3 for homework, using the present
...onditional to give advice. Collect the responses and correct the grammar
...) For further practice, offer exercises from *Focus on Grammar, High
...liate,* and *Understanding and Using English Grammar.* See the
...r Book References on pages 231–232 of the Student Book for specific
... chapters.

...orthStar: Reading and Writing

...s are also using the companion text, have them use the grammar
... on page 60 and change several of the present unreal conditionals in
...cises to past unreal conditionals.

...ting Politely to Ask Questions

...inutes 🕐

...dents practice interrupting to ask for clarification in a polite way, a
...unction that will be used in the Speaking Topic, page 65.

...closed, ask students what they would say to interrupt someone in
...a question. Write down the students' responses on the board. Then
... pen the books and read the introductory explanation and the
...ressions used to make a polite interruption. Ask students to
...list with the expressions on the board and discuss any differences
...tween them. Then have student pairs complete the exercise. Read through the
directions with the students. Have Student A in each pair read the first three
statements, deliberately making mistakes as described in the book. Student B
should ask for clarification about the items or anything else that is unclear, using
the polite phrases that were presented earlier. Monitor the pairs, listening for
usage of the polite phrases to make interruptions. Switch roles after statement 3.

Expansion/Homework

You may want to have one pair model the exercise for the class to make sure
everyone understands the procedure. They can role-play the example in the book
or create a new exchange.

For extra listening practice, use the NorthStar Companion Video.

✪✪✪D SPEAKING TOPIC

Suggested Time: 40 minutes 🕐

Focus

To give students a chance to use the knowledge, vocabulary, and skills they have
learned in the unit to arrive at a compromise solution to a problem through
group discussion.

Setup

Read the situation statement together. Then divide students into three groups (hospital administrators, interns, and patients' rights group). Allow students some time (about ten minutes) to clarify their points of view for Step 1, and to brainstorm what they will say in the role play for Step 2. Then, for Step 3, divide the class into new groups of three, with each student playing one of the roles. Have the groups role-play a meeting to discuss the situation, with instructions to reach a compromise that will satisfy everyone. For Step 4, have students discuss the same situation using the guiding questions on page 67, and explore whether the same problem exists in other professions. Finally, for Step 5, have groups summarize their meetings, giving their recommendations.

Expansion/Homework

Have students prepare both a news report of their meeting and an editorial from one perspective, and compare how their word choice differs between news and opinion.

✪E ▮ RESEARCH TOPIC

Suggested Time: 30 minutes ⊕

Focus

To interview people outside of class about their sleep habits.

Setup

Read the directions with the students. Have students take the survey on page 68 themselves. Ask them to think of two additional people they want to interview. After the surveys are complete, have students report back to the class on the responses they obtained, and their experience conducting the survey. Tally the responses to look for patterns. Finally, have students draw conclusions about sleep behavior based on their surveys.

Expansion/Homework

(1) If students do not have access to English speakers to interview, they can conduct the interviews in their native languages and translate the results for the presentation. (2) You may want to give the students some specific requirements regarding whom they interview. For example, you can ask some students to interview a young person (18–39 years old), some to interview a middle-aged person (40–64 years old), and others to interview an older person (over 65 years old). Or you could ask some students to interview men and others to interview women. Then groups could be formed that contain students who interviewed people of different ages or gender, and comparisons could be made about sleep habits.

Link to *NorthStar: Reading and Writing*

If students are also using the companion text, encourage them to include several questions in their survey about the ailments mentioned on page 66 to see if they find any correlation between attitudes toward sleep and attitudes toward treatment of illness.

The Eye of the Storm

OVERVIEW

Theme:	Natural Disasters
Listenings:	Listening One: *Preparing for a Hurricane* A radio news report Listening Two: *Hurricane Hunters* A radio news report
Critical Thinking Skills:	Use context clues to guess meaning Analyze a speaker's emotions Infer word meaning from context Hypothesize another's point of view Make judgments Support opinions with information from the reports
Listening Tasks:	Listen to a report with static interference Relate previous knowledge to the listening Identify chronology in a report Identify a speaker's emotions Summarize main ideas Listen for specific information Identify intonation patterns in speech Listen to student reports and take notes Watch a disaster movie and take notes
Speaking Tasks:	Make predictions Share personal experiences and fears Construct and perform a dialogue Express surprise, shock, and interest in news Present an emergency weather report Conduct an interview Present a movie review
Pronunciation:	Listing intonation
Vocabulary:	Context clues Word definitions Synonyms Word forms
Grammar:	Adjective clauses

UNIT SUMMARY

This unit focuses on the experience of preparing for and surviving a hurricane from the perspectives of residents, tourists, government officials, and scientists. Listening One is a radio report on preparing for and surviving a hurricane. Listening Two is an in-flight interview with the Hurricane Hunters (scientists who fly into the eye of a hurricane to gather data).

The companion unit of *NorthStar: Reading and Writing* deals with the eyewitness stories of people who have survived natural disasters.

1 Focus on the Topic, PAGE 69

✪✪✪A PREDICTING

Suggested Time: 10 minutes ⏱

Focus
To get students to use the picture and title to predict the type of disaster that will be discussed in the unit.

Setup
Have students work in pairs (of different language backgrounds, if possible) to look at the picture and discuss their answers. As a class, elicit answers from several of the students, trying to get a variety of responses. To encourage discussion, write down some of the suggested meanings for the title.

Expansion/Homework
You can also discuss these questions as a class without doing the pair work first. Try to elicit opinions from a variety of students, and encourage students to discuss the ideas with each other.

✪✪B SHARING INFORMATION

Suggested Time: 20 minutes ⏱

Focus
To encourage free discussion of the different types of disasters common around the world.

Setup
Assign students (from different geographical regions, if possible) to small groups. Have students discuss their answers. After completing question 3, you can have the groups come together as a class and discuss which types of disasters the students have experienced.

Expansion/Homework
Although this topic can promote a great deal of animated discussion, you need to be sensitive to the fact that some students may have lost a family member,

home, or business as a result of a natural disaster. You should preface the exercise by finding out if anyone has survived a serious disaster, and then be tactful during class discussions.

✪✪✪ C   PREPARING TO LISTEN

BACKGROUND
Suggested Time: 30 minutes 🕐

Focus
To introduce the topic of hurricanes by exploring students' knowledge of the phenomenon; to preview the vocabulary necessary for understanding Listening One.

Setup
Have students read the introductory information individually or as a class. Go over the descriptions on page 71, explaining vocabulary as necessary. Have students do the matching activity, and then compare their answers in pairs (with a student sitting nearby). Discuss any questions students have as a class.

VOCABULARY FOR COMPREHENSION
Suggested Time: 15 minutes 🕐

Focus
To introduce vocabulary and concepts related to hurricanes and natural disasters to aid listening comprehension.

Setup
Have students read the story and do the matching activity individually. Then pair them up (to a classmate sitting nearby) to check their answers. As a class, go over the answers and practice pronouncing the vocabulary items.

Expansion/Homework
To save time, you can assign the exercise as homework and use class time to work on pronunciation and check answers.

② Focus on Listening, PAGE 73

✪✪✪ A   LISTENING ONE: *Preparing for a Hurricane*
Suggested Time: 10 minutes 🕐

Focus
To encourage students to make predictions about the content of the radio report; to become familiar with the speakers' voices.

Setup

Read the introductory paragraph and the beginning of the statements with the students. Play the audio, stopping after each excerpt to allow students to fill in their predictions. Elicit ideas from several students about how each sentence will be completed in the report. Affirm each prediction as a possibility.

✪✪✪ LISTENING FOR MAIN IDEAS
Suggested Time: 15 minutes ⏱

Focus

To help students identify the topics discussed in the report by putting them in the correct order.

Setup

Have students read the list of topics. Play the report once while they number the topics in the order they occur. Check the answers by asking students the order and writing it on the board, allowing students to discuss any discrepancies with each other before you supply the correct answer.

✪✪✪ LISTENING FOR DETAILS
Suggested Time: 15 minutes ⏱

Focus

To get students to listen for specific details in the report.

Setup

Have students read the items and answer the questions they know. Play the report, and have students circle the answers. If needed, play the audio again. Have student pairs (of different listening abilities, if possible) compare answers. If disagreements arise, replay those segments rather than simply giving the answer.

Expansion/Homework

You can have students revisit their predictions from the first part of Listening One, page 74. In particular, they can compare questions 1 and 2 on page 75 of this section to prediction questions 2 and 3 on page 74.

✪✪ REACTING TO THE LISTENING
Suggested Time: 30 minutes ⏱

Focus

To get students to infer a speaker's confidence from listening to paralinguistic features (e.g., speed, pitch, pauses, laughter).

Setup

For Exercise 1, read through the directions, and model by repeating one sentence in several different manners to show how the way we speak can communicate as much meaning as the words we speak. Then have students listen to the excerpts, assign a place on the confidence scale for each speaker, and identify the speech features that influenced their decision in each case. For Exercise 2, have students discuss the questions in small groups. Write vocabulary items from Vocabulary for Comprehension, pages 72–73, on the board if desired, and encourage students to use the vocabulary in their discussions. Then have the class discuss how the disaster preparation advice and media coverage would be different for earthquakes and other disasters and why.

Expansion/Homework

After Exercise 2 is completed, you can ask the class as a whole to identify which disasters are the most difficult to plan for and why.

✪✪✪ B   LISTENING TWO: *Hurricane Hunters*

Suggested Time: 20 minutes ⏱

Focus

To learn about a method scientists use to study hurricanes.

Setup

Look at the title, and ask students to predict what it means. Then have them read the questions. Play the report as students answer the questions, repeating the listening as necessary. Ask students to compare answers in pairs (with a student sitting nearby) before checking the answers as a class.

✪✪✪ C   LINKING LISTENINGS ONE AND TWO

Suggested Time: 30 minutes ⏱

Focus

To get students to use the information they have heard to construct a short dialogue; to get students to react and respond to the listenings.

Setup

For Exercise 1, divide students into pairs (of different language backgrounds or language levels, if possible). In Step 1, have them brainstorm questions for use in the dialogue. In Step 2, have the pairs make up a dialogue between a hurricane hunter and a local authority. List the vocabulary from Vocabulary for Comprehension, pages 72–73, on the board to encourage students to use it in the dialogues. Have students perform the dialogues for the class. Take notes for later error correction. Then have the students discuss the questions in Exercise 2 in pairs or small groups.

Link to *NorthStar: Reading and Writing*

If students are also using the companion text, you can focus instead on the experience of surviving a hurricane. Have students make up a dialogue between a news reporter and the survivor of a hurricane. The reporter can ask questions about how the victim prepared for the hurricane and what happened during the storm. The victim can describe the experience of surviving a hurricane, drawing on the information in the two readings.

🔳 Focus on Vocabulary, PAGE 79

✪ EXERCISE 1
Suggested Time: 20 minutes 🕐

Focus
To help students understand and use past and present participles as adjectives in sentences.

Setup
Write two example sentences on the board to show the difference between the adjective forms (e.g., *I was frightened during the hurricane. The hurricane was frightening.*). Explain the difference between describing how a person feels and describing the cause of the feeling. Have the students complete the sentences. Check the answers by asking each student to read one sentence. Discuss any errors.

Expansion/Homework
(1) To save time, you can assign this exercise as homework, and use class time to read the items out loud and check the answers. (2) To check the students' understanding individually, you can ask them to write sentences for homework about a natural disaster they experienced, using three pairs of adjectives from the exercise. Then have students write their sentences on the board for the whole class to discuss, or you can review them yourself.

Link to *NorthStar: Reading and Writing*
If students are also using the companion text, you can ask them to pair the present participle adjectives from pages 79–80 of this unit with the nouns on page 79 of *Reading and Writing*.

✪ EXERCISE 2
Suggested Time: 30 minutes 🕐

Focus
To review vocabulary from the listening; extend students' ability to use the words by completing dialogues.

Setup
Have students work in pairs for both dialogues. First have Students A and B choose the correct words to complete the statements in their respective sections. For this exercise, Student A should look at page 81, and Student B should look at page 225 in the Student Book. Before starting the exercise, have one pair of students model the first two items in the exercise so everyone understands how it works. Have Student A start the dialogue, reading the first sentences and filling in the missing text with a word from the box above. Then Student B checks Student A's answer and reads the next sentence. After the scripted dialogues are completed, students should continue on their own, using any of the vocabulary words in the boxes on page 81.

Expansion/Homework

To save time in class, you can have students fill in the statement blanks as homework, using class time to check the answers and do the dialogues.

Link to *NorthStar: Reading and Writing*

If students are also using the companion text, you can write the adjectives (e.g., *sweltering*) from Focus on Vocabulary, page 78, of that book on the board, and ask students to use them in their dialogues.

 For extra vocabulary practice, have students work on the self-grading vocabulary activities for the unit on the NorthStar Companion Website at **http://www.longman.com/northstar**.

4 Focus on Speaking, PAGE 82

❋❋A   PRONUNCIATION: Listing Intonation

Suggested Time: 15 minutes

Focus

To have students practice using listing intonation to communicate more effectively in the Speaking Topic, page 90.

Setup

Read through the explanation and examples together. Then, in Exercise 1, have students listen to the sentences and mark the intonation pattern. Have them read the sentences aloud, following the intonation they've marked, and then listen to the audio once more to compare their reading with the model. For Exercise 2, have students complete the lists for each category and then practice reading their lists with a partner. Listen to the students' reading, and correct intonation as necessary. Have students remain in pairs for Exercise 3. Students take turns asking and answering the questions. Remind students to answer with an unfinished list (rising intonation).

❋❋B   GRAMMAR: Adjective Clauses

Suggested Time: 50 minutes

Focus

To have students practice adjective clauses, a grammatical point that will also be used in the Speaking Topic, page 90, while discussing natural disasters.

Setup

Discover students' existing knowledge by having them read the sentences and answer the questions in Exercise 1. Present the grammar point, referring students to the grammar box on pages 84–85. For Exercise 2, have student pairs (of different fluency levels, if possible) fill in the relative pronouns, then take turns reading the warnings to each other. For the Guessing Game in Exercise 3, divide the class into two groups. Tell students in Group A to look at page 87, while students in Group B look at page 226 in the Student Activities section of the student book. Have both groups look at their clues for the Guessing Game and fill in the appropriate relative pronouns. Then have Group A give their clues, while Group B guesses the words. When all the words have been guessed, have Group B give their clues.

Expansion/Homework

(1) Exercise 2 can be done as homework, using class time to check answers and complete Exercise 3. (2) To check the students' grammar individually, you can ask them to choose five words from Vocabulary for Comprehension, pages 72–73, and write clues for them. Collect the clues and correct the grammar. (3) For further practice, offer exercises from *Focus on Grammar, High Intermediate,* and *Understanding and Using English Grammar.* See the Grammar Book References on pages 231–232 of the Student Book for specific units and chapters.

✪✪✪ C   **STYLE: Expressing Surprise and Shock**

Suggested Time: 30 minutes

Focus

To help students practice using phrases to express surprise and shock, a useful function when discussing natural disasters.

Setup

With books closed, ask students what they would say if someone told them something very surprising. Write the students' responses on the board. Then open the books, and read the introduction and list of phrases to express surprise and shock. Discuss the difference between surprise and shock, and clarify any other vocabulary that students have questions about. Ask students to look at the list on the board, and discuss any differences between the phrases. Pronounce the phrases, and ask students to listen to how your tone of voice changes (e.g., more emotion when expressing strong surprise or shock). Then have pairs (of similar fluency levels, if possible) do the exercise, taking turns reading the comments and expressing mild surprise, disbelief, or shock. Circulate and help students with intonation.

For extra listening practice, use the NorthStar Companion Video.

✪✪✪ D · SPEAKING TOPIC

Suggested Time: 30 minutes

Focus

To give students a chance to use the knowledge, vocabulary, and skills they have learned in the unit to create disaster warning announcements.

Setup

Read the directions with the students. Divide students into pairs (of different language backgrounds, if possible). Let the pairs work together in class to write the announcements, giving assistance as needed. The announcements can either be performed in class, or audio- or videotaped outside of class and played the next day. As students listen, have them take notes on what type of disaster the warning is about and what advice is given. Take notes for error correction.

Expansion/Homework

(1) To make a guessing game out of this activity, you can write the names of different disasters on slips of paper and have the pairs pick their disaster at random. Instruct the students to write their warnings with detailed suggestions and instructions, without mentioning the name of the disaster. Then, while listening, the other students can take notes and try to guess which disaster each warning is about. (2) For a more light-hearted activity, you can instruct students to use funny sound effects and wear costumes while performing their announcements (e.g., a student giving a warning about the blizzard can dress in mittens, a scarf, and a hat).

✪ E · RESEARCH TOPICS

Activity 1: Conducting an Interview
Suggested Time: 30 minutes

Focus

To have students use the information and ideas they have learned in the unit to conduct an interview with someone who has experienced a disaster.

Setup

Help students to identify someone they can interview. As a class, brainstorm some questions that students can ask during the interview. Tell students to take notes about the story they hear. After the interviews, have students meet in small groups of four or five to recount the disaster stories they heard.

Activity 2: Watching a Disaster Movie
Suggested Time: 30 minutes ⏱

Focus
To help students use their new understanding of disasters to watch and analyze a popular movie.

Setup
Preview the movie you choose. Have students read the questions first. Show the film in lab hours, or go to a movie theater. Follow up with small-group discussions and reports by students on particular questions.

Expansion/Homework
(1) You may want to write down snippets of dialogue from the movie that contain idiomatic expressions and useful vocabulary relating to the unit— disaster preparation or expressions of surprise and shock—and help students use the context to guess the meaning. (2) Have students analyze why these movies are so popular.

Link to *NorthStar: Reading and Writing*
If students are also using the companion text, you can have students focus on the experience of the survivors. They can take notes on the different emotions of the survivors as the movie progresses.

You Will Be This Land

OVERVIEW

Theme:	Conservation

Listenings:	Listening One: *Interview with a Medicine Priest*
	     A conversation with a Cherokee spiritual leader
	Listening Two: *Ndakinna—A Poem*
	     An Abenaki poem

Critical Thinking Skills:	Interpret quotations Draw conclusions Support generalizations with examples Evaluate situations according to criteria set forth in the listening Infer information not explicit in the interview Hypothesize another's point of view Evaluate personal conservation efforts Analyze symbolism in a poem
Listening Tasks:	Summarize main ideas Listen for details Relate personal experience and values to the listening Take dictation Compare and contrast viewpoints in the listenings Identify sounds Listen for specific information Listen to and ask questions about student research
Speaking Tasks:	Make predictions Express opinions Interview a classmate Read aloud or recite a poem Ask for and give examples Role-play a meeting Use new vocabulary to assess personal conservation habits Report research findings
Pronunciation:	*th* sounds
Vocabulary:	Word definitions Synonyms Context clues Word forms
Grammar:	Advisability in the past—past modals

UNIT SUMMARY

This unit focuses on a Native American perspective on protecting the environment and how traditional Native American beliefs about nature can be applied to modern life. Listening One is an interview with David Winston, a Cherokee medicine priest, who describes Cherokee spiritual beliefs regarding the environment and conservation. Listening Two is a poem about the Earth by Joseph Bruchac, a member of the Abenaki tribe.

The companion unit in *NorthStar: Reading and Writing* deals with urban development and the environment, and planning to create ecology-friendly cities.

1 Focus on the Topic, PAGE 91

✪✪✪ A PREDICTING

Suggested Time: 10 minutes ⏱

Focus

To get students thinking about the image of the Earth as our "home"; to use the unit title to predict the content of the unit.

Setup

Have student pairs (of different language backgrounds or language levels, if possible) look at the picture and discuss the questions. Then as a class, elicit answers from several of the students, trying to get a variety of opinions. To encourage discussion, write several of the predictions about the topic of the unit on the board.

Expansion/Homework

You can also discuss these questions as a class without doing the pair work first. Try to elicit responses from a variety of students and encourage them to discuss the questions with each other.

✪✪ B SHARING INFORMATION

Suggested Time: 20 minutes ⏱

Focus

To encourage discussion of environmental problems and solutions.

Setup

Have small groups of three or four students (of different language backgrounds, if possible) discuss the quotations and match each to its meaning.

Expansion/Homework

Have students share proverbs or quotations about nature from their native languages.

✦✦✦ C █ **PREPARING TO LISTEN** ███████████████████████████████

BACKGROUND
Suggested Time: 30 minutes ⊕

Focus
To introduce the students to some aspects of traditional Native American religions; to explore the importance of eagles and other animals in Native American religious beliefs.

Setup
Have students read the introductory passage individually in class or at home as homework. As a class, discuss the passage, particularly the use of the eagle as a symbol in the Pawnee religion. Have pairs answer the questions, then come together again as a class to share responses.

Expansion/Homework
(1) To save time, assign the introductory passage as homework, using class time to discuss the questions. Because the Pawnee story is symbolic, you may need to spend some time with students to help them interpret it. Read the story out loud to the students. Then ask them to explain in their own words the symbolism represented by the eagle's two wings, feathers, and ability to look in two directions. (2) When discussing question 2, you may encounter some inaccurate information from students about Native Americans, such as stereotypical images from old "cowboy and Indian" movies. Encourage students first to identify the information they have learned about Native Americans, then to evaluate its accuracy.

Link to *NorthStar: Reading and Writing*
If students are also using the companion text, you can ask them to speculate about how traditional Native Americans would feel about the ecovillage introduced on page 89 of that text.

VOCABULARY FOR COMPREHENSION
Suggested Time: 15 minutes ⊕

Focus
To introduce vocabulary and concepts related to conservation and religions to aid listening comprehension.

Setup
Have students work individually to read the sentences and choose the synonymous expressions without using a dictionary. Then have them exchange books or papers with a nearby student to check each other's answers. Check the answers as a class, and go over the pronunciation of the vocabulary items.

Expansion/Homework
To save time, you can assign the matching exercise as homework, and use class time to check on pronunciation and answers.

2 Focus on Listening, PAGE 95

✪✪✪A LISTENING ONE: *Interview with a Medicine Priest*

Suggested Time: 10 minutes 🕐

Focus

To encourage students to make predictions about the Cherokee spiritual beliefs; to become familiar with David Winston's voice.

Setup

Ask students to read the introductory paragraph and the prediction questions. Then play the excerpt from the interview, and allow students time to write answers to the questions. Next have them discuss their answers in pairs (of different fluency levels, if possible). Elicit predictions from several students, affirming each prediction as a possibility.

✪✪✪ LISTENING FOR MAIN IDEAS

Suggested Time: 15 minutes 🕐

Focus

To help students identify the three laws of nature explained by David Winston.

Setup

Have students read the questions. Play the interview once without stopping while students take notes. Have students compare their notes with those of a partner before checking the answers as a class.

✪✪✪ LISTENING FOR DETAILS

Suggested Time: 15 minutes 🕐

Focus

To get students to listen for specific details in the interview.

Setup

Have students read the items and answer the questions they know. Then play the interview and have students complete the exercise. If students seem to have trouble, play the interview one more time. Allow them to compare their answers in pairs before going over the answers as a class. If disagreements arise, replay those segments rather than simply giving the answers.

✪✪ REACTING TO THE LISTENING

Suggested Time: 20 minutes 🕐

Focus

To encourage a deeper understanding of the three laws of nature by getting students to hypothesize about how they would apply in different situations.

Setup

For Exercise 1, have students read the instuctions. Then ask them to look at the actions listed on the chart for Excerpt One. Play Excerpt One, stopping the audio to allow students time to mark their answers. Replay the excerpt as needed. Repeat this procedure for the other excerpts. During the discussions get students to give reasons for their answers. Emphasize that it is possible for students to have varying opinions as long as their reasoning is sound. For Exercise 2, have students discuss the questions in small groups (of different fluency levels, if possible). As these questions focus on students' individual experiences and opinions, remind students to be sensitive to each other.

Expansion/Homework

(1) You may want students to listen to the excerpts a second time and take notes to help them explain why they chose a particular answer. (2) If students are interested, allow them to continue their discussion about the native people in their home countries as a class.

✪✪✪ B LISTENING TWO: "Ndakinna"—A Poem

Suggested Time: 50 minutes 🕑

Focus

To present another Native American perspective on nature and conservation; to expose students to a different type of listening—a poem.

Setup

Read through the statements in Exercise 1 with the students. Play the poem once. Encourage them to listen not only to the words but also to the mood of the poem. After listening, have students compare their answers (with a nearby student) and discuss them as a class. However, don't give them a correct answer—this is a prediction exercise. Do the same for Exercise 2. For Exercise 3, have students read the text of the poem before listening and filling in the missing words. Replay the poem as needed. Check the answers with the class. Then have students read the poem with its completed sentences, and listen again.

Expansion/Homework

(1) You may want students to listen to the poem once before looking at Exercises 1 and 2. With books closed, ask students to listen to the poem and write down one or more adjectives describing the feeling they get while they listen. Write the adjectives on the board and discuss them briefly. Then have students open their books and proceed with Exercise 1.

✪✪✪ C LINKING LISTENINGS ONE AND TWO

Suggested Time: 30 minutes 🕑

Focus

To get students to synthesize the information they learned about Native American spiritual beliefs; to infer opinions based on the interview and poem.

Setup

Review the quotations on page 100, and see if students have changed their initial opinions based on the information they have learned. Then ask students to decide how David Winston and Joseph Bruchac might feel about the same quotations. Students can refer to their summaries of the Three Laws of Nature on page 96 and the text of the poem "Ndakinna" on page 99 to help them decide. Then have students discuss their choices in groups. You may want to list the vocabulary from Vocabulary for Comprehension, pages 94–95, on the board to encourage students to use it in their discussions.

Expansion/Homework

At the end of his interview, David Winston says "The Great Life can live without us, but we can't live without the Great Life." Ask students to paraphrase this quotation. Write all the paraphrases on the board and discuss their similarities and differences.

Link to *NorthStar: Reading and Writing*

If students are also using the companion text, you can ask them to hypothesize about how ecocities and earthship homes would fit into the Cherokee belief system. Have them discuss how acceptable both practices would be under the three Laws of Nature.

3 Focus on Vocabulary, PAGE 100

✪ EXERCISE 1
Suggested Time: 15 minutes 🕐

Focus

To review and extend students' understanding of vocabulary from the listenings by using different word forms.

Setup

Have pairs (of different fluency levels, if possible) complete the word-form chart in Exercise 1 and then check the chart as a class. Be sure that students have access to dictionaries for this exercise.

Expansion/Homework

This can be done as homework, so that class time can be used to check answers.

✪ EXERCISE 2
Suggested Time: 15 minutes 🕐

Focus

To have students practice using different word forms in context; to give and support opinions.

Setup

Have student pairs complete the paragraphs with the appropriate word forms from the chart; then discuss whether they agree or disagree with the statements. Encourage students to use word forms as they discuss their opinions, in order to get more practice using the vocabulary during unstructured communication.

Expansion/Homework

This exercise can be completed as homework, so class time can be used to check answers and discuss the students' opinions about the statements.

✪ EXERCISE 3
Suggested Time: 15 minutes 🕐

Focus

To have students evaluate the environmental impact of various items.

Setup

Show students how to complete the chart using the model given. Students complete the chart individually or with a partner. Then have students take turns discussing their answers with a partner.

Expansion/Homework

Have partners decide which of the items causes the greatest harm to the environment, and which the least. Compare answers as a class, encouraging students to support their opinions with examples.

 For extra vocabulary practice, have students work on the self-grading vocabulary activities for the unit on the NorthStar Companion Website at **http://www.longman.com/northstar**.

▉4 Focus on Speaking, PAGE 104

✪✪A PRONUNCIATION: *th* Sounds
Suggested Time: 40 minutes 🕐

Focus

To help students understand and learn to use the English *th* sounds.

Setup

Introduce students to the two *th* sounds. Then play the pronunciation exercise as students circle the words they hear in Exercise 1. After checking their answers, have students practice pronouncing the words in pairs (from different language backgrounds, if possible) for Exercise 2. Monitor the students and make corrections as necessary. Encourage a playful atmosphere by showing that it is the tongue tip that goes between the teeth, not the whole tongue (though it may feel that way to students!). For Exercises 3–5, students can continue with the same partner. For Exercise 4, Student A should look at page 105 and read the clues, while Student B uses the list of words on page 227 of the Student Book to guess the answer. When Student A has read all the clues, it is Student B's turn to give clues. For Exercise 5, go back to Listening Two on the audio. Have students look at the text of the poem on page 99 and underline all the *th* sounds they hear. Then have them practice reading the poem, paying special attention to the *th* sounds.

Expansion/Homework

(1) Before doing Exercise 2, you can replay Exercise 1 on the audio and have students repeat the words after the speaker. (2) To check students' pronunciation individually, you can have students record themselves reading the words from Exercise 1 and the poem on page 99. Listen to their recording, and give students feedback on their pronunciation.

✪✪ B   GRAMMAR: Advisability in the Past—Past Modals

Suggested Time: 50 minutes 🕐

Focus

To have students practice using past modals to express regret and blame, a grammatical point that will be used in the Speaking Topics, page 110.

Setup

Discover students' existing knowledge by having them answer the questions in Exercise 1. Then present the grammar, referring students to the grammar box on page 106. Have students complete Exercise 2, then have pairs (of different language backgrounds or language levels, if possible) read the story out loud. Check the answers by asking each pair to read one sentence out loud, while other students listen and make corrections. For Exercise 3, read through the directions and example dialogue with the students. Then have students discuss the items on the Personal Environmental Report and give themselves a grade, explaining what they could have done better. Monitor the pairs for usage and pronunciation of the past modals.

Expansion/Homework

(1) To check the students' grammar individually, you can ask each student to write for homework a list of things they could have done in the past month to protect the environment. Collect the lists and correct the grammar. (2) For further practice, offer exercises from *Focus on Grammar, High Intermediate,* and *Understanding and Using English Grammar.* See the Grammar Book References on pages 231–232 of the Student Book for specific units and chapters.

Link to *NorthStar: Reading and Writing*

If students are using the companion text, they can also use expressions of blame and regret in their discussions in Exercise 3 (e.g., *I know I should've taken public transportation, but it's not my fault. The city should've made better bus routes!*).

✪✪✪ C   STYLE: Asking For and Giving Examples

Suggested Time: 30 minutes

Focus

To help students practice asking for and giving examples, a function that will be used again in the Speaking Topics, page 110.

Setup

With books closed, ask students what they would say to ask someone for an example to illustrate what the person is saying. Write the students' responses on the board. Then open the books, and read the introductory paragraph, the excerpt from David Winston's interview, and the example expressions with the students. Ask students to compare the examples to the list on the board, and discuss any differences. Then put students in small groups of three or four to discuss environmental programs sponsored by the government or community where they live. Remind them to give specific examples to illustrate their descriptions.

Expansion/Homework

(1) Before starting the exercise, you may want to brainstorm a list of environmental programs that students can refer to (e.g., recycling, sewage treatment, nature preserves, limits on building). (2) To incorporate more practice with past modals, you can also ask students to describe a policy that has hurt the environment, giving examples of the negative effects and describing what should have happened instead.

 For extra listening practice, use the NorthStar Companion Video.

✪✪✪ D   SPEAKING TOPICS

Activity 1: Role Play
Suggested Time: 50 minutes

Focus

To give students a chance to use the information, vocabulary, and skills they have learned in the unit to develop a role play about an environmental problem.

Setup

Read through the situation and roles with the students. Help assign students to roles, and have students who will be playing the same role (e.g., all the medicine priests) meet together to work on their part. Encourage students to get into character, deciding how each person would argue his or her point in the meeting. Emphasize that, at this point, students should focus on developing opinions of their character and not try to resolve the problem. If they wish, students can take notes to help them in the next step. Then regroup for the role play. Remind students that each character in the role play should express his or her opinion, and that while they should work for compromise, no one should suddenly change his or her position in an unrealistic way. Monitor the groups to make sure everyone is participating and also to correct errors. After the role plays are finished, reconvene as a class for a group discussion on how students felt in their roles and the solutions that groups came up with.

Expansion/Homework

To save time in class, you can ask students to read the situation and roles for homework.

Activity 2: Writing a Poem About Nature
Suggested Time: 30 minutes 🎧

Focus

To use new vocabulary to compose a poem about nature.

Setup

Read through the directions with the students. Let students choose a partner. If possible, bring in (or have them bring in) other pictures of nature to look at while they write. Allow students to use a dictionary or thesaurus, and help them correct grammar and vocabulary usage. After the poems are finished, have students perform them for the class.

Expansion/Homework

You may want to have students record their poems. Offer feedback on pronunciation and phrasing.

Activity 3: Reading a Poem About Nature
Suggested Time: 30 minutes 🎧

Focus

To find, read, analyze, and explain a poem about nature.

Setup

Read through the directions with the students. Help them find a poem by suggesting the names of some famous poets or bringing some books of poetry to class. Have students work in pairs or small groups to discuss a poem, using dictionaries to help them with new vocabulary. Help students practice reciting the poem with appropriate pronunciation (each student in the pair or group can recite a portion of the poem). Have each student present a poem to the class, first reciting and then explaining it.

Expansion/Homework

To give students some individual feedback on their recitation, you can ask them to record the poem individually. Then listen to their recording, and give them feedback on their pronunciation and phrasing.

✪**E** ▌**RESEARCH TOPIC**

Suggested Time: 30 minutes ⏲

Focus

To find quotations by or about Native Americans or indigenous people.

Setup

Read through the directions with the students. Explain how to search a quotations dictionary, or review how to do an Internet search, if necessary. Have students present their quotations to the class and explain what they learned during their research.

Expansion/Homework

Have students work in pairs (of different fluency levels, if possible) or small groups to do the research, using dictionaries to help them with new vocabulary.

It's Better to Give Than to Receive

OVERVIEW

Theme:	Philanthropy

Listenings:	Listening One: *Oseola McCarty*
	    A report on the life of a philanthropist
	Listening Two: *Please Donate or Volunteer*
	    Two public service announcements

Critical Thinking Skills:	Make judgments Identify personal assumptions about philanthropy Correlate abstract principles with concrete examples Hypothesize rationales for philanthropic actions Critique public service announcements Compare and contrast information Rank desirable employee qualities
Listening Tasks:	Identify main ideas Listen for details Listen and take notes using a graphic organizer Synthesize information from both listenings Interpret speakers' intent by analyzing intonation Listen to and evaluate student presentations Research a charitable organization or philanthropist through telephone inquiries
Speaking Tasks:	Make predictions Express and support opinions with examples Construct and perform a dialogue Use new vocabulary to discuss examples of charitable efforts Ask for clarification using tag questions Use gambits that indicate priorities Develop and perform a public service announcement Report research findings
Pronunciation:	Intonation of tag questions
Vocabulary:	Context clues Word definitions Synonyms
Grammar:	Tag questions

UNIT SUMMARY

This unit examines the motivations, ranging from altruistic to selfish, of people who give money to charity. Listening One is a news report about Oseola McCarty, a woman who washed laundry for a living but managed to save $250,000, which she gave away to a university scholarship fund. Listening Two contains public service announcements urging people to donate money or to volunteer for various causes.

The companion unit of *NorthStar: Reading and Writing* deals with the benefits that volunteers (particularly young people) receive from donating their time and energy to a charity.

1 Focus on the Topic, PAGE 113

✪✪✪ A PREDICTING

Suggested Time: 10 minutes

Focus
To get students thinking about what kind of people donate time and money, and why; to use the title to predict the unit content.

Setup
Have students work in pairs (of different language backgrounds, if possible) to discuss and answer the questions. As a class, elicit answers from several of the students. For question 1, probe a bit to get students to explain their responses to Jimmy Carter's volunteer work and try to get a variety of opinions.

Expansion/Homework
You can also discuss these questions as a class without doing the pair work first. Try to elicit opinions from a variety of students and encourage students to discuss their answers.

✪✪ B SHARING INFORMATION

Suggested Time: 20 minutes

Focus
To encourage free discussion of philanthropists and causes they support.

Setup
Have students work in small groups of three or four (of different language backgrounds, if possible). After students read the definition of philanthropy, have them discuss the questions. Then come together as a class and ask the groups to briefly report back on one of the questions. (Question 2 or 4 would work well.)

✪✪✪ C | **PREPARING TO LISTEN**

BACKGROUND
Suggested Time: 30 minutes 🕐

Focus
To give some background on philanthropy in the United States; to explore some reasons why individuals and corporations make donations.

Setup
Have students read the introduction, or read it to them as a listening. Put students in small groups (of different language backgrounds or language levels, if possible) to do the exercise. Have students read the list of reasons for donating money and add any other reasons they can think of. Then have them read the three newspaper clippings and decide what the donor's reasons are for giving, emphasizing that they may have more than one. Come together as a class and have the groups present their ideas about the donations.

Expansion/Homework
To save time, you can assign the introduction as homework, using class time to do the exercise.

Link to *NorthStar: Reading and Writing*
If students are also using the companion text, you can ask them to compare the reasons for volunteering versus donating money. Use the example of Jimmy Carter in the opener, and refer also to the quotations on page 112 of *Reading and Writing*. Ask students to decide whether any of the reasons on page 115 of *Listening and Speaking* would apply to Carter's volunteer work and to think of any additional reasons why he might do volunteer work instead of donating money. You could also make a comparison by looking at the reasons expressed by volunteers on pages 113–114 of *Reading and Writing*.

VOCABULARY FOR COMPREHENSION
Suggested Time: 15 minutes 🕐

Focus
To introduce vocabulary and concepts relating to philanthropy to aid listening comprehension.

Setup
Have students work individually to read the pamphlet and complete the matching task without a dictionary. Then have them compare their answers with a student sitting nearby. Have that pair of students compare their answers with another pair. As a class, go over the answers and practice pronunciation of the underlined words.

Expansion/Homework
To save time, you can assign the matching exercise as homework and use class time to check pronunciation and answers.

② Focus on Listening, PAGE 118

PAGE 118

✪✪✪ **A** ▌ LISTENING ONE: *Oseola McCarty—An Unusual Philanthropist*

Suggested Time: 10 minutes ⏱

Focus
To encourage students to make predictions about Oseola McCarty.

Setup
Have students look at the picture of Oseola McCarty and read the questions. Play the excerpt from the news report and elicit predictions. Then elicit answers to the questions from the class, affirming each as a possibility.

Expansion/Homework
Have students write down their predictions, share them with a partner, then discuss them with the class.

✪✪✪ **LISTENING FOR MAIN IDEAS**

Suggested Time: 15 minutes ⏱

Focus
To help students listen for the main ideas in the news report.

Setup
Have students read the statements. Then play the news report once while students mark the statements T or F. Have students compare their answers in pairs (of different language levels, if possible) before checking them with the class.

Expansion/Homework
You can also ask the pairs to write corrections for the false statements.

✪✪✪ **LISTENING FOR DETAILS**

Suggested Time: 15 minutes ⏱

Focus
To help students listen for specific details in the news report.

Setup
Have students read the items and answer the questions they know. Play the news report again, and have students complete the statements. If needed, play the report again. Go over the answers. If disagreements arise, replay the segments rather than simply giving the answers.

✪✪ **REACTING TO THE LISTENING**

Suggested Time: 20 minutes ⏱

Focus
To encourage students to make inferences about Oseola McCarty's motivation for her donation, based on her statements in the news report.

Setup

For Exercise 1, have students read the list of possible reasons for donating money. Then play the excerpts, stopping after each one to give students time to write their answers. Emphasize that there can be more than one right answer, as long as the students' reasoning is sound. Replay the excerpts as needed. Allow students to compare their answers in pairs before discussing the answers as a class. For Exercise 2, have students discuss the questions in small groups (of similar fluency levels, if possible). During the discussion, ask students to give specific examples from the excerpts to support their answers.

✪✪✪ B LISTENING TWO: *Please Donate or Volunteer—Public Service Announcements*

Suggested Time: 20 minutes 🕑

Focus

To extend students' understanding of philanthropy by analyzing advertisements asking people to give money or volunteer for a cause; to expose students to a different kind of listening.

Setup

Introduce the idea of public service announcements by reading the introduction with the students. Have students look at the chart in Exercise 1. Play the first PSA, stopping to allow students to write their answers. Replay the PSA as needed. Ask students to compare their answers with those of another student (of a different language level, if possible) and discuss the answers with the class. Repeat the procedure with the second PSA. Then have students get into small groups for Exercise 2.

Expansion/Homework

(1) Before playing Listening Two, you may want to take a moment to briefly mention the U.S. Constitution, which is mentioned in the first PSA as a means of invoking the American ideal of "freedom." Explain that students will hear a reference to the Constitution, the document describing the rules and regulations of the United States, including the First Amendment of the Bill of Rights, which guarantees Americans freedom of religion, speech, the press, and assembly.
(2) Since students will have a more difficult time listening for why people should volunteer, you may want to play the PSA once, asking students to fill in only the left-hand column of the chart. Then play the PSA again for students to fill in the right-hand column.

✪✪✪ C LINKING LISTENINGS ONE AND TWO

Suggested Time: 30 minutes 🕑

Focus

To get students to reflect on Oseola McCarty's gift and to compare the reasons behind her gift with the reasons people are encouraged to give in the PSA announcements.

Setup

Have students fill in the Venn diagram with information from both listenings. Refer students back to their answers to the exercises for Listenings One and Two.

Link to *NorthStar: Reading and Writing*

If students are also using the companion text, you can ask them to look again at Reading One, pages 115–118, to find similarities and differences between the motivations for Oseola McCarty's and Justin Lebo's philanthropic work.

3 Focus on Vocabulary, PAGE 122

✪ EXERCISES 1–3
Suggested Time: 30 minutes

Focus

To expand understanding and usage of vocabulary from the listenings by completing a newspaper article and then making up a dialogue.

Setup

For Exercise 1, pronounce the vocabulary items and have the students repeat them. Then have the students fill in the missing vocabulary in the newspaper article. Have students compare their answers with someone sitting nearby and then check them as a class. Have student pairs (of similar fluency levels, if posssible) do Exercise 2. After reading the newspaper article, have them write and practice a dialogue using at least ten of the vocabulary items. As pairs perform their dialogues for the class, have the other students listen and check off the vocabulary items they hear. For Exercise 3, have students work in pairs and discuss the charitable organizations, using the vocabulary in the box. Encourage students to make eye contact as they listen and comment.

Expansion/Homework

(1) To save time, you can have students do Exercise 1 for homework. (2) You can have the student pairs record their comments and listen to them, taking notes on the vocabulary usage and giving feedback to the students.

Link to *NorthStar: Reading and Writing*

If students are also using the companion text, you can write the vocabulary from Vocabulary for Comprehension, pages 114–115, on the board and ask students to use those words in their dialogues as well.

 For extra vocabulary practice, have students work on the self-grading vocabulary activities for the unit on the NorthStar Companion Website at **http://www.longman.com/northstar**.

4 Focus on Speaking, PAGE 125

✪✪ A PRONUNCIATION: Intonation of Tag Questions

Suggested Time: 15 minutes ⏱

Focus
To help students understand how intonation conveys meaning in tag questions; to practice tag question intonation patterns.

Setup
Have students read the introduction and examples, or read it to them as a listening. For Exercise 1, have students listen to the sentences, draw intonation lines, and decide if the speaker is really asking a question or just making a comment. For Exercise 2, have students read the dialogue in pairs. Before reading aloud, have students go through the dialogue together, deciding whether tag questions should have rising or falling intonation.

Expansion/Homework
Have students re-read the dialogue, using opposite intonation for the tag questions (turning comments into questions and questions into comments). Discuss how the change in intonation changes the meaning conveyed by the speakers, even when the words remain the same.

✪✪ B GRAMMAR: Tag Questions

Suggested Time: 50 minutes ⏱

Focus
To have students practice distinguishing and using tag questions to make a comment or ask a question, a grammatical point that will be used in the Speaking Topic, page 132.

Setup
Review what students know about tag questions by having two students read the dialogue in Exercise 1 aloud. Discuss answers to the questions as a class. Present the grammatical point, referring students to the grammar box on pages 127–128. For Exercise 2, have partners fill in the tag questions in Step 1. In Step 2, play the recorded conversation while students mark the intonation of the tag questions. Remind them that falling intonation indicates that the tag is a comment (not requiring a real answer), while rising intonation indicates that the tag is a question. Then, for Step 3, have pairs of students (from different language backgrounds or language levels, if possible) practice the dialogue together. For Exercise 3, Step 1 have students read the statements and underline the "false" information. For Step 2, have students take turns asking tag questions to check information. In Step 3, write the correct information in Step 1.

Expansion/Homework

(1) After students fill in the tag questions in Step 1 of Exercise 2, you can ask them to look carefully at the responses and mark the tag questions with rising or falling intonation. They can check the intonation in Step 2. (2) To check your students' grammatical usage individually, you can ask them to look back at the "Teddy Bear Lady" story on page 123 and write as homework three question-type tag questions and three comment-type tag questions, marking them with the correct intonation. Collect the questions, and correct the grammar. (3) For further practice, offer exercises from *Focus on Grammar, High Intermediate,* and *Understanding and Using English Grammar.* See the Grammar Book References on pages 231–232 of the Student Book for specific units and chapters.

✪✪✪ C   STYLE: Prioritizing or Ranking Ideas

Suggested Time: 30 minutes

Focus

To help students use expressions to prioritize or rank ideas, a function that will be used again in the Speaking Topic, page 132, by discussing the qualities necessary for a volunteer.

Setup

Have students read the introductory statement and the phrases in the box. Ask them to add any other phrases they know. Then divide the students into groups (of different language levels, if possible) to do the exercise. For Step 1, have students read the ads. For Step 2, have students discuss the personal qualities necessary for each job using expressions from the box and tag questions when possible. Monitor the students' discussions for usage of the target phrases.

Expansion/Homework

To encourage students to use the target phrases to express and ask for opinions, you may also want to have a student in each group tally how many times the other students use the phrases during the discussion.

  For extra listening practice, use the NorthStar Companion Video.

✪✪✪ D   SPEAKING TOPIC

Suggested Time: 50 minutes

Focus

To give students a chance to use the knowledge, vocabulary, and skills they have learned in the unit to create a public service announcement for a not-for-profit organization.

Setup

Read the directions with the students or have the students read silently. Divide the class into groups of three (of different language levels, if possible). Help each group select an organization and a target audience. Before students start to write their ads, emphasize that everyone should have a speaking part and that students should be creative—using humor, sound effects, and anything else they can think of to make the ad catchy and interesting. Then have the groups record the announcements. Play the announcements in class or in the language lab, and have the groups vote (but not for their own group) to select the most interesting and most convincing PSAs. Offer written feedback on the content and language of the ad.

Expansion/Homework

(1) If possible, students can perform their PSAs on videotape, which would allow the use of costumes or other visuals, or they can perform them in class. (2) To encourage students' creativity, you can have two simple prizes (such as a special certificate or some candy), which you can award for the best PSAs. You can also assign one organization and target audience to the whole class or to several groups; groups with a PSA for the same organization compete, and other students vote on the best one.

Link to *NorthStar: Reading and Writing*

If students are also using the companion text, you can make a connection to the readings by asking at least one group to choose high school students as their target audience, and asking another group to write a PSA to encourage people to donate old bicycles for Justin Lebo's bicycle rebuilding project.

✪E   RESEARCH TOPICS

Activity 1: Researching an Organization or a Philanthropist
Suggested Time: 30 minutes ⏱

Focus

To find out more about a not-for-profit organization or a philanthropist.

Setup

Have students (in pairs or as individuals) choose an organization or person to research. They can choose from the list in the book, but encourage them to investigate a person or organization that supports a cause they believe in. If students have access to the Internet, they can visit The Foundation Center's Web site (www.fdncenter.org). It has links to many philanthropic organizations, both in the United States and internationally. (Click on the "Searchzone" link on their home page, then search by topic.) After they complete the research, have students give a brief presentation on what they learned to the class. Offer feedback on content and language.

Activity 2: Visiting a Volunteer Organization
Suggested Time: 30 minutes ⏸

Focus
To find out about a local organization that relies on volunteer workers and to make a presentation about it.

Setup
Have students visit a local organization in pairs or alone. Then help them identify an organization and call to make an appointment to speak to someone about their volunteer programs. As a class, brainstorm some additional questions that students can ask about. After the visits, have students report back to the class and discuss the organizations.

Expansion/Homework
(1) To encourage students to listen to each other's reports and to give feedback to the speakers, you can ask students to evaluate each other's presentations (or assign each speaker three evaluators, spreading the evaluations out equally). Ask each student to evaluate the research and presentation skills separately (rating each one *Excellent, Very Good, Good,* or *Poor*), writing down one thing they especially liked about the presentation and one thing that could be improved.
(2) You can also evaluate in the same manner (but perhaps in more detail), and give each speaker a copy of your evaluation and the peer evaluations.

Link to *NorthStar: Reading and Writing*
If students are also using the companion text, you can link the topics by helping students develop questions to find out whether the person they interview would support mandatory volunteering.

Emotional Intelligence

OVERVIEW

Theme:	Education

Listenings:	Listening One: *Can You Learn EQ?*
	    A psychology radio program
	Listening Two: *Test Your EQ*
	    An emotional intelligence test

Critical Thinking Skills:	Interpret a cartoon
	Define notions of intelligence
	Identify and evaluate assumptions about intelligence
	Hypothesize another's point of view
	Connect principles of emotional intelligence to specific
	    behaviors
	Interpret quotations
	Analyze past encounters according to principles of emotional
	    intelligence

Listening Tasks:	Preview a listening Take notes while listening using a graphic organizer Listen for details Provide information from the listening to support answers Relate listening to personal experiences Integrate information from both listenings Listen to classmates' stories and take notes Listen to and evaluate student responses Watch and analyze student role plays
Speaking Tasks:	Make predictions Support opinions with examples Compose and perform a dialogue using new vocabulary Recount an emotional experience Use opening gambits to restate information for clarification or emphasis Restate quotations Perform a role play Conduct an interview
Pronunciation:	Unstressed vowels
Vocabulary:	Context clues Synonyms Idiomatic expressions
Grammar:	Direct and indirect speech

This unit focuses on emotional intelligence (EQ), a theory of intelligence that emphasizes such emotional skills as self-awareness and empathy, rather than the analytical skills normally associated with "intelligence." Listening One is an interview with two educators, who give their opinions on the role of emotional intelligence and whether EQ can be learned. Listening Two contains a discussion of the answers to an EQ test.

The companion unit of *NorthStar: Reading and Writing* deals with advantages and disadvantages of home schooling.

1 Focus on the Topic, PAGE 135

✪✪✪ A PREDICTING

Suggested Time: 10 minutes ⏱

Focus
To get students thinking about a definition of intelligence by reacting to a stereotypical "mad scientist" image.

Setup
Have student pairs (of different language backgrounds or language levels, if possible) look at the picture and discuss the questions. Then, as a class, elicit answers to the questions from several of the students, trying to get a variety of responses.

Expansion/Homework
You can also ask students to discuss whether or not they think the cartoon gives an accurate picture of a scientist or if it is just a stereotype. If you have a class with students who have a variety of academic or professional backgrounds (e.g., science majors and art majors, or engineers and salesclerks), you can pair students with dissimilar backgrounds in order to provoke more discussion of the cartoon.

✪✪ B SHARING INFORMATION

Suggested Time: 20 minutes ⏱

Focus
To encourage free discussion of the qualities and abilities of an intelligent person.

Setup

Have students look at the photographs, and be sure everyone is familiar with the people pictured. Have students discuss their answers to question 1 in small groups (of similar fluency levels, if possible). Then ask the groups to share their responses. As a class, review the students' opinions about which people they considered intelligent, especially if they mention different ways of being intelligent. Then have students work in groups again to discuss question 2.

✪✪✪ C   PREPARING TO LISTEN

BACKGROUND
Suggested Time: 20 minutes

Focus
To explore the history of intelligence testing and criticism of the IQ test; to examine students' opinions about intelligence.

Setup
Have students read the passage individually. Then have students complete the opinion survey and discuss their answers in small groups.

Expansion/Homework
To save time, you can assign the introduction as homework, using class time to complete and discuss the survey.

Link to *NorthStar: Reading and Writing*
If students are also using the companion text, you can ask them the following question: *Do you think an IQ test would be a good way to measure whether a child was learning enough in home schooling? Why or why not?*

VOCABULARY FOR COMPREHENSION
Suggested Time: 15 minutes

Focus
To introduce vocabulary and concepts relating to emotions and intelligence to aid listening comprehension.

Setup
Practice pronunciation of the underlined words. Then have students complete the task individually before comparing their answers with those of a student sitting nearby. Go over the answers as a class.

Expansion/Homework
To save time, you can assign the vocabulary exercise as homework and use class time to work on pronunciation and check answers.

2 Focus on Listening, PAGE 139

✪✪✪ A | LISTENING ONE: *Can You Learn EQ?*

Suggested Time: 10 minutes ⏱

Focus

To encourage students to make predictions about the interview's content and participants; to become familiar with the voice of the interviewer.

Setup

Have students read the questions. Play the excerpt from the interview and give students a few moments to compare their answers in pairs (of different fluency levels, if possible) before eliciting predictions from the class. Affirm each prediction as a possibility.

Expansion/Homework

Have students write down predictions, share them, and then discuss their ideas with the class.

✪✪✪ LISTENING FOR MAIN IDEAS

Suggested Time: 20 minutes ⏱

Focus

To help students listen for the opinions of each person interviewed.

Setup

Have students look at the chart. Play the audio once as students take notes to fill in the chart. Have students compare their answers in pairs before checking them with the class.

✪✪✪ LISTENING FOR DETAILS

Suggested Time: 15 minutes ⏱

Focus

To help students listen for specific details of the interview.

Setup

Have students read the items and predict qualities a person with high EQ might have. Then play the news report, stopping between each part, and have students check off qualities they hear mentioned. Allow the students to compare answers in pairs, replaying the report as needed. Go over the answers as a class. If disagreements arise, replay the segments rather than simply giving the answers.

✪✪ REACTING TO THE LISTENING

Suggested Time: 20 minutes ⏱

Focus

To encourage students to extend their understanding of Emotional Intelligence by applying the theory to specific examples from the interview.

Setup

For Exercise 1, have students read the instructions and the list of five skills included in Emotional Intelligence. Discuss the skills to make sure they are clear to the students. Play the excerpts, stopping after each one to allow students to write their answers. Replay the excerpts as needed. Then, in small groups or as a class, have students compare and discuss their answers. Emphasize that there can be more than one answer as long as the students' reasoning is sound. For Exercise 2, have students discuss the questions in small groups (of similar fluency levels, if possible).

Expansion/Homework

To help students understand the five skills, you may want to ask them to give you examples of a time they used one of the skills to solve a problem. Start by giving an example from your own experience (e.g., *Once I had a student who never did his homework. I used my people skills to talk to him about the problem. When I found out that he didn't understand the material, I used empathy to understand how he was feeling.*).

✪✪✪ B LISTENING TWO: *Test Your EQ*

Suggested Time: 30 minutes 🕐

Focus

To extend students' understanding of Emotional Intelligence by having them take an EQ test and listen to a discussion of the answers.

Setup

For Exercise 1, have students read the EQ test and answer the questions. Emphasize that they should choose the answer that best describes what they would do in the situation. For Exercise 2, play the interview while students listen for the "high EQ answer" and take notes on why it is the best answer. Replay the interview as needed. Go over the answers as a class.

✪✪✪ C LINKING LISTENINGS ONE AND TWO

Suggested Time: 30 minutes 🕐

Focus

To get students to reflect on and react to the theory of Emotional Intelligence.

Setup

Divide students into small groups (of different language backgrounds, if possible) to discuss the questions. Then have them report highlights of the discussion to the class. Encourage the use of vocabulary from Vocabulary for Comprehension, pages 137–138, by listing it on the board.

Link to *NorthStar: Reading and Writing*

If students are also using the companion text, you can ask them to discuss how home schooling would affect the development of EQ. Have them refer to the five skills of Emotional Intelligence on page 141 of the Student Book, while they look at Reading One, "Teaching at Home Hits New High with Internet," pages 142–144, in *Reading and Writing*. Ask students to find examples of how the five skills of Emotional Intelligence are, or are not, developed during home schooling.

❸ Focus on Vocabulary, PAGE 144

✪ EXERCISES 1–3
Suggested Time: 30 minutes 🕐

Focus
To practice using words and phrases from the listenings that describe emotional traits; to discuss qualities necessary for different jobs.

Setup
For Exercise 1, have students review the list of words and phrases as a class, clarifying the meaning of any they are unsure about. Then have students work in pairs (of different fluency levels, if possible) to complete the statements. Check the answers briefly with the class. For Exercise 2, question 1, the pairs can continue working together to describe the qualities needed in their chosen job. Then have each pair report back on one of the jobs and ask other students to respond to their descriptions. For Exercise 2, question 2, have students discuss their own emotional experiences in small groups. Circulate and encourage students to use language from this unit in their discussions. Have students who are willing share their best stories with the class.

Expansion/Homework
To check students' understanding of the vocabulary, for homework you can ask students to choose three jobs from Exercise 2, question 1, and write a short paragraph on each, using the vocabulary words.

 For extra vocabulary practice, have students work on the self-grading vocabulary activities for the unit on the NorthStar Companion Website at **http://www.longman.com/northstar**.

❹ Focus on Speaking, PAGE 146

✪✪ A   PRONUNCIATION: Unstressed Vowels
Suggested Time: 30 minutes 🕐

Focus
To help students understand and practice the unstressed vowel *(schwa)* sound.

Setup

Write the example words on the board. Introduce the *schwa* sound, helping students to pick out the syllables that are unstressed and modeling the pronunciation. Exaggerate the sound to help students relax and enjoy the exercise. Then play Exercise 1 while students put slashes between the syllables. Play Exercise 1 again as they mark the syllables with the strongest stress and the *schwa* sound. Play the list of words again for Exercise 2, as students repeat the words aloud. Put students in pairs (from different language backgrounds, if possible) for Exercise 3. Have them listen and mark the stressed vowels in each multisyllable word in the advertisement. Then have each student practice reading the advertisement aloud to his or her partner. Monitor the students and correct their pronunciation.

Expansion/Homework

To check students' pronunciation individually, you can have them record the advertisement. Listen to the recordings and then record your feedback, modeling corrections for them on the tape.

✪✪ B   GRAMMAR: Direct and Indirect Speech

Suggested Time: 40 minutes 🕘

Focus

To have students practice using direct and indirect speech, a grammatical point that will be used in the Speaking Topics, page 151.

Setup

In Exercise 1, have students read the examples and answer the questions. Discover the students' knowledge of the grammar by eliciting answers from the class. Present the grammar on pages 148–149. For Exercise 2, have pairs (of different language abilities, if possible) model the activity with the first item. Student B responds to the statement using indirect speech, and Student A says whether Student B is correct. Students switch roles after item 4.

Expansion/Homework

(1) To give students more practice, you can ask them to make up some additional statements and restatements and check for indirect speech. (2) To check students' grammatical usage, write several sentences on the board using direct speech (you may want to include sentences with the verb tenses and modals included in the grammar box). Have students restate the sentences in indirect speech for homework. Collect the papers, and either make corrections or turn their examples into an exercise for class correction. (3) For further practice, offer exercises from *Focus on Grammar, High Intermediate,* and *Understanding and Using English Grammar.* See the Grammar Book References on pages 231–232 of the Student Book for specific units and chapters.

✪✪✪ C ▐ **STYLE: Restating for Clarification or Emphasis**

Suggested Time: 30 minutes ⏱

Focus

To help students restate quotations in their own words, a function that will be used again in the Speaking Topics and Research Topic, pages 151–154.

Setup

Introduce restating by putting the quotation by Blaise Pascal on the board. Ask students what they think it means, and then jot down a few of their answers. Then look at the example of the students' interpretation. Explain that when you restate, you express an idea in your own words. You can contrast this with how the quotation would be rephrased using indirect speech (e.g., Blaise Pascal said that the heart has its reasons which reason knows nothing of). Have students read the list of phrases to begin a restatement, and then look at the example conversation again. Before beginning the exercise as a class, ask students to look at the quotations individually and write down some notes about what they think each means. Then ask students to share their ideas about the quotes, calling on different students for their interpretations. To encourage discussion, assign one or two students to be note takers, writing on the board the restatements that they hear for each quote during the discussion. Monitor the students to make sure they are using the introductory phrases.

Expansion/Homework

(1) Before the class discussion, you may want to have student pairs come up with restatements first. You can discourage students from simply restating the quotes by telling them that they should not use any of the content words in their paraphrases (words other than *but, and, if, so, the*, etc.). Encourage them to find synonyms by looking in a thesaurus. (2) To give individual feedback, you can ask students to restate one or two of the quotations as homework. Give feedback on the form and content of their restatements.

 For extra listening practice, use the NorthStar Companion Video..

✪✪✪ D ▐ **SPEAKING TOPICS**

Activity 1: Role Play
Suggested Time: 50 minutes ⏱

Focus

To give students a chance to use the knowledge, vocabulary, and skills they have learned in the unit to create a role play.

Setup

Read the directions, and give the students time to read through the roles. Have pairs (of similar language abilities) choose a role. Emphasize that each person should either play the part of someone with a high EQ (who has all the skills discussed in the unit) or a low EQ (who doesn't have the skills). During the role plays, have the audience members take notes to answer the questions in question 2, and then have the class discuss question 2 after each role play. Remind students to give specific examples, using indirect speech and restating, to discuss what was said in the role plays.

Expansion/Homework

(1) You can ask the pairs to prepare two role plays: one in which the characters have low EQ skills, and one in which they have high EQ skills. Ask audience members to write down things that the characters did differently in the two role plays. (2) Students can also record or videotape their role plays to be watched in class or in the language lab. Offer written feedback on form or content.

Link to *NorthStar: Reading and Writing*

If students are also using the companion text, you can add a role play on the theme of home schooling. Write the following situation on the board and encourage students that choose this role play to refer to Unit 7 of *Reading and Writing* for more inspiration for their roles.

Situation: A mother and a father.

Student A: You want to teach your two young children at home. You believe that the schools do not give good academic preparation and you could do better. You are willing to quit your job in order to stay at home and teach your children. Your husband/wife doesn't agree with you.

Student B: You want your children to attend school. You think that they will miss learning a lot of social skills if they are taught at home. Also, you don't want your husband/wife to stop working because you need the money.

Activity 2: Create an EQ Test
Suggested Time: 30 minutes ⏱

Focus

To give students a chance to use the knowledge, vocabulary, and skills they have acquired during the unit to create an EQ test.

Setup

Review the five EQ skills in Reacting to the Listening, page 141, and the EQ test, pages 142–143. Have small groups write their own version of the test. Then have each group discuss their test with another group.

Expansion/Homework

You can have students "take" the EQ tests written by the other groups before having a discussion.

✪E RESEARCH TOPIC

Suggested Time: 30 minutes

Focus

To help students get other perspectives on the theory of Emotional Intelligence.

Setup

Help students think of someone to interview about emotional intelligence. Preferably, it should be someone they admire or someone who will have an interesting perspective on the subject. Have small groups of students (of different language abilities, if possible) prepare an explanation of emotional intelligence, since the person they interview may not have heard about the theory. First have them prepare a short statement outlining the theory. You could have them start the sentence "Emotional Intelligence is . . ." Encourage them to look back at the unit and use their restating skills from pages 150–151 to introduce their definition of the theory. Then have them come up with examples to illustrate each of the five skills. They can choose examples from the unit or think of their own. After the explanation of EQ is completed, students can conduct the interviews using the questions on page 154. Have each student give a brief presentation reporting on the information he or she learned in the interview. Remind them to use indirect speech and restating to report what the person said in the interview.

Link to *NorthStar: Reading and Writing*

If students are also using the companion text, you can add a question about home schooling to the interview. Add the following to the list between questions 4 and 5 on page 154: *Some children are taught at home instead of going to school. Do you think this is a good way to prepare people for your profession? What would be the advantages and disadvantages?*

Goodbye to the Sit-Down Meal

OVERVIEW	
Theme:	Food

Listenings:	Listening One: *French Sandwiches*
	    A radio news report
	Listening Two: *Food in a Bowl*
	    A conversation about food trends

Critical Thinking Skills:	Identify and analyze food trends Relate general factors to specific behaviors Interpret meaning from text Compare traditional and contemporary food practices Infer word meaning from context Compare and contrast two restaurants Infer situational context
Listening Tasks:	Summarize main ideas Listen for details Interpret speaker's tone and attitude Relate the listening to local food trends Classify vowel sounds Listen to student food shows and evaluate using a rubric Listen to a food show on TV
Speaking Tasks:	Make predictions Share ideas on food trends Use tone of voice to indicate attitude in a role play Use new vocabulary in free conversation Compose and perform a dialogue Practice gambits which call attention to a particular item Explain how to use a tool Develop and perform a food show Report research on food trends
Pronunciation:	Spelling and sounds: *oo* and *o*
Vocabulary:	Context clues Synonyms Definitions Figurative meanings of words Vocabulary classification Idiomatic expressions
Grammar:	Phrasal verbs

UNIT SUMMARY

This unit focuses on changing trends in eating habits. Listening One is a report on changing eating habits in France. Listening Two is a report on a fast-food trend.

The companion unit of *NorthStar: Reading and Writing* deals with cooking processes, traditions, superstitions, and religious beliefs involved with eating.

1 Focus on the Topic, PAGE 155

✪✪✪A PREDICTING

Suggested Time: 10 minutes 🕐

Focus
To get students thinking about the way they eat, and whether their habits have changed in the past decades.

Setup
Have student pairs (of different language backgrounds or language levels, if possible) look at the cartoon and discuss the questions. Then, as a class, elicit answers to the questions from several of the students, trying to get a variety of responses.

Expansion/Homework
You can also ask students to share what they have had for meals over the previous day or week.

✪✪B SHARING INFORMATION

Suggested Time: 20 minutes 🕐

Focus
To encourage free discussion of the six factors that influence food trends.

Setup
Have students look at the diagram, and be sure everyone is familiar with the factors identified. Have students read and answer the questions individually, and then discuss their answers in small groups (of similar fluency levels, if possible). If desired, ask the groups to share their responses.

✪✪✪ C | PREPARING TO LISTEN

BACKGROUND
Suggested Time: 20 minutes 🕙

Focus
To explore the traditional image of the long French lunch, and compare that with modern reality.

Setup
Have students read the passage individually. Then have students work in small groups to discuss traditional versus modern meals in their own cultures.

Expansion/Homework
To save time, you can assign the introduction as homework, using class time for discussion.

Link to *NorthStar: Reading and Writing*
If students are also using the companion text, you can ask them to explain their most memorable meal. Was it traditional? If so, was it in connection with a holiday? Or, was it modern? If so, what made it memorable?

VOCABULARY FOR COMPREHENSION
Suggested Time: 15 minutes 🕙

Focus
To introduce vocabulary and concepts relating to food and eating habits to aid listening comprehension.

Setup
Practice pronunciation of the underlined words. Then have students complete the task individually before comparing their answers with those of a student sitting nearby. Go over the answers as a class.

Expansion/Homework
To save time, you can assign the vocabulary exercise as homework and use class time to work on pronunciation and check answers.

2 Focus on Listening, PAGE 159

✪✪✪ A | LISTENING ONE: *French Sandwiches*
Suggested Time: 10 minutes 🕙

Focus
To encourage students to make predictions about the news report; to become familiar with the voices of the speakers.

Setup

Have students read the questions. Play the excerpt from the interview, and give students a few moments to compare their answers in pairs (of different fluency levels, if possible) before eliciting predictions from the class. Affirm each prediction as a possibility.

Expansion/Homework

Have students write down predictions, share them, and then discuss their ideas with the class.

✪✪✪ LISTENING FOR MAIN IDEAS
Suggested Time: 20 minutes ⏱

Focus

To help students listen for the main points from the report.

Setup

Have students look at the questions. Play the audio once, and allow time for students to write short answers to the questions. Have students compare their answers in pairs before checking them with the class.

✪✪✪ LISTENING FOR DETAILS
Suggested Time: 15 minutes ⏱

Focus

To help students listen for specific details in the report.

Setup

Have students read the items and answer the questions they know. Play the news report again, and have students circle the best answer to each question. Allow the students to compare answers in pairs, replaying the interview as needed. Go over the answers as a class. If disagreements arise, replay the segments rather than simply giving the answers.

✪✪ REACTING TO THE LISTENING
Suggested Time: 20 minutes ⏱

Focus

To help students understand double meaning in words; to discuss implications of the trend toward fast food.

Setup

For Exercise 1, read the instructions together, and provide a model to demonstrate double meaning in words (e.g., a person or the weather can be "cold"). Play the excerpts, stopping after each one to allow students to circle their answers. Replay the excerpts as needed. Then, in small groups or as a class, have students compare and check their answers. For Exercise 2, students discuss the questions in small groups (of different language backgrounds, if possible).

Expansion/Homework
Encourage students to share additional words they've heard used with double meaning, or to provide examples (with translation) from their own languages.

✪✪✪ **B** **LISTENING TWO:** *Food in a Bowl*

Suggested Time: 30 minutes 🕧

Focus
To extend students' understanding of food trends, this time the trend toward food in bowls.

Setup
Discover what students already know about the topic by asking them if fast food in their country includes meals in which all the ingredients are in one bowl. Then read through the introductory paragraph together. Play the audio, and have students circle the correct answer for each item. Replay the report as needed. Go over the answers as a class.

✪✪✪ **C** **LINKING LISTENINGS ONE AND TWO**

Suggested Time: 30 minutes 🕧

Focus
To get students to identify speakers by tone and style of speaking.

Setup
Have students look at the list of possible speakers, and predict how they might differ in style of speech. Go over the words to describe different speaking styles, and be sure students understand them. Then read each conversation aloud and have students identify the speaker and style. Replay conversations as needed, and allow time for students to write their answers.

Expansion/Homework
Have students record the conversations in pairs, and then play the conversations.

Link to *NorthStar: Reading and Writing*
If students are also using the companion text, you can ask them to discuss how Slow Food movement advocates might feel about both food trends highlighted in the listenings.

🔳 Focus on Vocabulary, PAGE 166

✪ **EXERCISES 1–3**
Suggested Time: 30 minutes 🕧

Focus
To practice using words and phrases from the listenings related to food and food trends.

Setup

For Exercise 1, have students review the list of words and phrases as a class, clarifying the meaning of any they are unsure about. Then have students complete the chart, and compare their answers in pairs. Check the answers briefly with the class. For Exercise 2, students match food idioms to their meaning. For Exercise 3, students take turns asking and answering questions with a partner. Circulate and encourage students to use language from this unit in their answers. For Exercise 4, have students who are willing share interesting stories from Exercise 3 with the class.

Expansion/Homework

To check students' understanding of the vocabulary, for homework you can ask students to choose idioms from Exercise 2 and write sentences using them.

 For extra vocabulary practice, have students work on the self-grading vocabulary activities for the unit on the NorthStar Companion Website at **http://www.longman.com/northstar**.

4 Focus on Speaking, PAGE 168

✪✪A   PRONUNCIATION: Spelling and Sounds—*oo* and *o*

Suggested Time: 30 minutes ⏱

Focus

To help students understand and practice words with *oo* and *o* sound-spelling patterns.

Setup

Write the example words on the board. Introduce the *oo* and *o* sounds, modeling the pronunciation. Then play Exercise 1, and have students circle the words with different vowel sounds. Play Exercise 1 again to allow students to check their answers, and have them practice saying the words with the audio. Play the list of *oo* words for Exercise 2, and have students repeat them. Then, with partners, have students write the words from the list under the appropriate sound. Students practice reading the words and correcting each other's pronunciation. Students do the same thing for the *o* words in Exercise 3. For Exercise 4, have students mark the correct vowel sound for each *oo* and *o* sound in the list (have students use phonetic symbols, or assign a number to each sound). Then have students take turns asking and answering the questions. Encourage students to use the listed words in their answers. Monitor the students, and correct their pronunciation as necessary.

Expansion/Homework

To check students' pronunciation individually, you can have them record the lists of words, and questions and answers. Listen to the recordings and then record your feedback, modeling corrections for them on the audio.

✪✪ B GRAMMAR: Phrasal Verbs

Suggested Time: 50 minutes 🕐

Focus
To have students practice using phrasal verbs, a grammatical point that will be used in the Speaking Topic, page 176.

Setup
Have student pairs (of similar language levels, if possible) read the examples and answer the questions in Exercise 1. Discover what students know about the grammar by having the class answer the questions. Present the grammar, referring students to the grammar box on pages 171–172. For Exercise 2, have students work in pairs to complete the telephone conversations using the phrasal verbs in parentheses. Check answers as a class by having students read lines from the conversations. For Exercise 3, have students match the phrasal verbs from the conversations with their definitions. For Exercise 4, have students work in groups of four (of similar language levels, if possible) to create a conversation, using phrasal verbs from this unit. After students have finished their conversations, have them role play for the class.

Expansion/Homework
(1) To check your students' grammatical usage individually, instead of correcting Exercise 3 as a class, you can ask students to complete it in writing for homework. Then collect the papers and make corrections. (2) For further practice, offer exercises from *Focus on Grammar, High Intermediate,* and *Understanding and Using English Grammar.* See the Grammar Book References on pages 231–232 of the Student Book for specific units and chapters.

Link to *NorthStar: Reading and Writing*
If students are also using the companion text, you can ask them to make a list of the phrasal verbs from *Reading and Writing*, pages 181–184. Assign two or three of the phrasal verbs to each pair and ask students to look them up in the dictionary to find out whether they are separable or inseparable.

✪✪✪ C STYLE: Calling Attention to a Particular Item

Suggested Time: 30 minutes 🕐

Focus
To help students focus an audience's attention on a particular item, a function that will be used again in the Speaking Topic, page 176.

Setup
Introduce how to focus by demonstrating with a classroom object (e.g., *Do you see what I'm holding?*). Ask students what word and phrases you used to focus their attention, and write down a few of their answers. Then look at the example and explanation in the book. Have students read the list of phrases to focus attention and then look at the example. Before beginning the exercise in groups, ask students to choose one of the items listed and think through how

they would demonstrate that item, using the listed phrases. Then, in small groups (of similar language levels, if possible), have students take turns explaining how to use their chosen utensil or gadget. Monitor the students to make sure they are using the attention-focusing phrases. Have students who are willing present their demonstration for the class.

Expansion/Homework

Videotape student demonstrations, and watch together. Help students identify ways they can use their body language to reinforce their attention-focusing phrases (e.g., direct eye contact, leaning toward the audience, pointing).

For extra listening practice, use the NorthStar Companion Video.

✪✪✪ D SPEAKING TOPIC

Suggested Time: 50 minutes

Focus

To give students a chance to use the knowledge, vocabulary, and skills they have learned in the unit to create an episode of a TV food show.

Setup

Ask students to share TV food shows that they are familiar with, either in the United States or in their home countries. Then for Step 1, have students decide what to demonstrate for their episode. For Step 2, students write a script for their demonstration. Write some of the phrasal verbs from page 174 and expressions from page 175 on the board, or direct students to those pages and remind them to include these phrases in their demonstrations. For Step 3, students perform their food show demonstrations for the class, or videotape the demonstrations and show the class at a later time. Finally, for Step 4, students use the chart to evaluate each other's episodes.

Expansion/Homework

(1) Set a time limit for students' food show episodes, to help keep them from becoming too detailed in their explanations. (2) Students can also watch the episodes and evaluate them in the language lab. Compile the evaluations and share the results with students.

✪ E RESEARCH TOPICS

Suggested Time: 30 minutes

Activity 1: Analyze Food Trends

Focus

To get students to analyze food trends in a local supermarket.

Setup

Elicit names of local supermarkets, and write them on the board. Have students identify which of the supermarkets they live near. Group students for the activity based on their proximity to the same supermarket. Before going to the supermarket, have students discuss trends that they anticipate finding. Then have students visit their assigned supermarket and answer the listed questions. Finally, have them prepare and report to the class on what they found.

Activity 2: Analyze a TV Food Show

Focus

To get students to analyze a TV food show based on the criteria introduced in this unit.

Setup

Go through the TV listings and identify TV food shows, noting the channel and time. Then, be sure that all students are either able to watch one of the food shows listed, or can watch at another student's home. Go over the questions students should be able to answer after watching the show, and encourage students to take notes while watching. Then have students use the questions to guide them in their analysis. Have students report back to the class.

Finding a Niche: The Lives of Young Immigrants

OVERVIEW	
Theme:	Immigration

Listenings:	Listening One: *A World Within a School*
	    A radio news report
	Listening Two: *The Words Escape Me*
	    A song

Critical Thinking Skills:	Compare personal experiences Recognize personal assumptions Hypothesize scenarios Infer word meaning from context Analyze language usage Compare and contrast two immigrant experiences Infer meaning not explicit in text Propose solutions
Listening Tasks:	Identify main ideas Listen for supporting details Interpret speaker's tone and pitch Relate the listening to personal values and interests Take a dictation Identify points of view in two listenings Classify sounds Listen to and comment on student plans
Speaking Tasks:	Make predictions Express opinions using new vocabulary Restate themes of the unit in a guided conversation Practice gambits to hesitate in response to a question Ask and answer questions about a chart Simulate a school board meeting Collaborate to develop an education plan Conduct an interview Compare interview results
Pronunciation:	Discriminating between *sh, z, ch,* and *j*
Vocabulary:	Context clues Synonyms Definitions Idiomatic expressions
Grammar:	Present and past—contrasting verb tenses

UNIT SUMMARY

This unit focuses on the experiences of young immigrants, particularly in school, and how they are affected by different philosophies about how immigrants should assimilate into a new culture. Listening One is a news report about teachers and students at the International High School in Queens, New York, where students are encouraged to maintain and develop their native languages and cultures. Listening Two is a song about one young person's experience coming to a new country.

The companion unit of *NorthStar: Reading and Writing* deals with the feelings of homesickness and nostalgia that many immigrants experience after moving to a new country.

1 Focus on the Topic, PAGE 179

✪✪✪A   PREDICTING

Suggested Time: 10 minutes ⏱

Focus
To get students thinking about the experience of immigrating to a new country; to use the title to predict the unit content.

Setup
Have students work in pairs (of different language backgrounds or language levels, if possible) to look at the picture and discuss the questions. As a class, elicit answers to the questions from several of the students, trying to get a variety of responses.

Expansion/Homework
You can also discuss these questions as a class without doing the pair work first. Try to elicit opinions from a variety of students and encourage students to discuss their answers with each other.

✪✪B   SHARING INFORMATION

Suggested Time: 20 minutes ⏱

Focus
To encourage free discussion about students' own immigration experiences and opinions about immigration.

Setup
Have students work in small groups (of different language backgrounds, if possible) to discuss the questions. Then ask students to share their results with the class. For question 2, elicit concerns from students and write them on the board to see if students share similar worries.

Expansion/Homework

After students have discussed their opinions for question 3, they can share their opinions as a class. Encourage students to support their opinions, but also to respect differing opinions.

Link to *NorthStar: Reading and Writing*

If students are also using the companion text, you can have them refer to the chart in that unit's Sharing Information, page 194. Students can look ahead at the list of countries in *Listening and Speaking*, page 181, and discuss how the reasons for immigrating may differ among people from different countries.

✪✪✪ C PREPARING TO LISTEN

BACKGROUND
Suggested Time: 20 minutes ⏱

Focus

To introduce some background on the challenges faced by teenage immigrants when they go to school in the United States and the types of schools that have been designed to meet their needs; to identify and discuss some of the countries with large immigrant populations in the United States.

Setup

Have students read the introduction individually. Then assign students to pairs (of different language backgrounds, if possible) to look at the map and discuss the questions.

VOCABULARY FOR COMPREHENSION
Suggested Time: 20 minutes ⏱

Focus

To introduce vocabulary and concepts relating to immigration and education to aid listening comprehension.

Setup

Have students pronounce the underlined words. Then pair them up (with a classmate sitting nearby) to read the sentences and then write a definition of the underlined words, without using a dictionary or looking at the matching exercise on page 183. Have each pair write one definition on the board. After the pairs match words with definitions in Exercise 2, have each pair correct or add to their definition on the board if necessary. Go over the answers as a class.

Expansion/Homework

To save time, you can assign the definitions as homework and use class time to work on pronunciation and check answers.

2 Focus on Listening, PAGE 184

✪✪✪ A   LISTENING ONE: *A World within a School*

Suggested Time: 10 minutes ⏱

Focus

To encourage students to make predictions about the International High School.

Setup

Have students read the questions, then listen to the excerpt from the report. Have students share their answers in pairs (of different language levels, if possible), and then elicit some predictions from the class. Affirm each prediction as a possibility.

✪✪✪ LISTENING FOR MAIN IDEAS

Suggested Time: 15 minutes ⏱

Focus

To help students listen for the main ideas in the news report.

Setup

Have students read the statements. Play the audio once only while students check the statements that are true. Have student pairs compare their answers before checking them with the class.

✪✪✪ LISTENING FOR DETAILS

Suggested Time: 15 minutes ⏱

Focus

To help students listen for the opinions expressed by people interviewed in the news report.

Setup

First, have students look at the chart. You may want to pronounce the names in the left-hand column so that students will be able to listen for them more easily. Then play the report again, and have students fill in the chart and then compare their answer with a partner. If needed, play the report again. Go over the answers as a class. If disagreements arise, replay the segments rather than simply giving the answers.

✪✪ REACTING TO THE LISTENING

Suggested Time: 20 minutes ⏱

Focus

To help students identify emphasized ideas based on pitch and length; to encourage students to share their feelings and opinions about the International High School.

Setup

For Exercise 1, have students look at the questions and possible areas of emphasis. Play the excerpts one at a time, stopping while students circle the idea being emphasized, and note the language features that help them understand the emphasis. Have students compare their answers in pairs, replaying the excerpts as needed. For Exercise 2, have students discuss the questions in small groups (of different language backgrounds, if possible). After the discussion, ask students to share some of their responses with the class.

✪✪✪ B   LISTENING TWO: *The Words Escape Me*

Suggested Time: 20 minutes 🕐

Focus

To extend students' understanding of immigration in the United States by listening to a song written from the perspective of a young immigrant.

Setup

Have students look at the questions and possible answers before listening. Then play the song once without pausing, to give students an overall context for the exercises. After listening, ask students to circle the answers. Replay the song as needed. Check the answers with the class. For Exercise 2, play the song again, and have students fill in the blanks. Check answers, and play the song once more to confirm.

Expansion/Homework

Reverse the order of Exercises 1 and 2. Have students fill in the song lyrics first, and then have them circle the meanings for particular lines.

✪✪✪ C   LINKING LISTENINGS ONE AND TWO

Suggested Time: 30 minutes 🕐

Focus

To get students to reflect on and react to what they have learned about U.S. immigration and the experience of young immigrants.

Setup

Divide students into small groups (of different language backgrounds, if possible.) Have them fill in the chart and then discuss their answers. Then have them write a role play based on their discussion. Encourage the use of vocabulary from Vocabulary for Comprehension, pages 182–183, by listing it on the board and referring students to it. Correct pronunciation and usage errors. Allow students to perform their role plays for the class.

Expansion/Homework

You can add a cross-cultural component by asking students to compare the International High School program and the "melting pot" and "salad bowl" philosophies to the situation of immigrants in another country with which they are familiar.

Link to *NorthStar: Reading and Writing*

If students are also using the companion text, you can ask them to think about how feelings of nostalgia and homesickness described in the readings can be addressed in a school setting. Have students refer to Linking Readings One and Two, page 204 of *Reading and Writing,* for a chart summarizing the themes addressed in both readings. Ask students: *Should teachers and school administrators do anything to help their immigrant students deal with the types of feelings expressed by the writers? If not, why not? If so, what should they do?*

❸ Focus on Vocabulary, PAGE 190

✪ EXERCISES 1–3
Suggested Time: 20 minutes ⏲

Focus
To review vocabulary from the listenings by reading a short passage about a young immigrant and selecting synonyms for selected vocabulary; to express personal opinions about immigration.

Setup
For Exercise 1, have students read the passage and do the matching individually. Then have students compare their answers in pairs (of similar language levels, if possible) before checking the answers with the class. Students can remain in pairs for Exercise 2. Have students read through each statement and decide how strongly they agree or disagree with it. Then have them explain their choices to their partners, using vocabulary from the list.

Expansion/Homework
To give more oral practice using the vocabulary, list the words from the reading on the board (along with additional words from Vocabulary for Comprehension, if you wish). Then ask the pairs to discuss the following questions, using the vocabulary as much as possible: (**1**) How might the adaptation process differ for immigrants of different ages (e.g., a young child, a teenager, a young adult, a middle-aged adult, and an elderly person)? (**2**) What can a person do to deal with feelings of culture shock? (**3**) Have you ever been in a place where you felt you didn't blend in? What was it like, and how did you deal with it?

Link to *NorthStar: Reading and Writing*
If students are also using the companion text, you can also include some of the vocabulary from that unit's Vocabulary for Comprehension, page 195.

 For extra vocabulary practice, have students work on the self-grading vocabulary activities for the unit on the NorthStar Companion Website at **http://www.longman.com/northstar**.

4 Focus on Speaking, PAGE 193

✿✿ A   PRONUNCIATION: Discriminating between *sh*, *z*, *ch*, and *j*

Suggested Time: 30 minutes ⏰

Focus
To help students distinguish between and practice the sounds.

Setup
Put the example words from the bottom of the box on page 193 on the board, and pronounce them. Draw attention to the target sounds, introduce the corresponding phonetic symbols, and explain how to produce the sounds. Then have students listen to Exercise 1 as they check off the sound they hear in each word. Check their answers, and then replay the exercise as students repeat the words after the speaker on the audio. For Exercise 2, have students work in pairs (of different language backgrounds, if possible). Have Student A read the statement or question, and then have Student B respond using the words provided in parentheses, switching roles after item 6. Remind students to pay attention to their pronunciation of the target sounds, and monitor the pairs as they work, making corrections as needed.

Expansion/Homework
(1) Students can give themselves a self-test of this pronunciation point by marking the sounds in Exercise 1 before they listen, and then listening to the audio and correcting their choices. (2) To check students' pronunciation individually, you can have students record the list of words on page 194 and the responses to the statements on page 195. Listen to the recordings and record your feedback, modeling corrections for them on the tape.

✿✿ B   GRAMMAR: Present and Past—Contrasting Verb Tenses

Suggested Time: 50 minutes ⏰

Focus
To have students practice using present and past verb tenses appropriately, a grammatical point that will be useful in the Speaking Topic, page 203.

Setup
In Exercise 1, have students work in pairs (of different language abilities) to read the examples and answer the questions. Discover the students' knowledge of the grammar by eliciting answers from the class. Present the grammar on pages 196–197. For Exercise 2, have the pairs choose the appropriate verb forms to complete the interview. To check the answers, have the students take turns reading the interview out loud, one sentence at a time, while the other students listen and make corrections. Then have the pairs do Exercise 3. Have Student A ask the questions using the appropriate verb tense, and then have Student B answer. Encourage Student A to ask follow-up questions to get more information about Student B's answers, especially for the more open-ended questions. Have students switch roles after question 6. Monitor the pairs and correct their verb-tense errors as necessary.

Expansion/Homework

(1) For more practice with the verb tenses, you can ask the pairs to discuss their response to the opinions expressed in the story, giving specific examples to illustrate their ideas while being careful to use the appropriate verb tenses. Then they can choose one opinion and write a short response to it. Students can exchange paragraphs to appreciate each other's work, then give them to you to check. (2) To check your students' grammatical usage individually, you can have them complete Exercise 3 in writing as homework (after they have done it orally in class). Then collect the papers and make corrections. You can also create an error correction exercise from their own work. (3) For further practice, offer exercises from *Focus on Grammar, High Intermediate,* and *Understanding and Using English Grammar.* See the Grammar Book References on pages 231–232 of the Student Book for specific units and chapters.

✪✪✪ C STYLE: Hesitating in Response to a Question

Suggested Time: 30 minutes

Focus
To help students learn to hesitate, or stall for time, when asked for an opinion—a function that can be used in the Speaking Topic, page 203.

Setup
With books closed, ask students what they say when someone asks a question and they need time to think before answering. Write the phrases on the board. Then have students open their books and read the introductory statement and the phrases in the box. Have them write down phrases from the board that don't appear in the box. For Exercise 1, have students circle the expressions that show hesitation. Have them compare answers with a partner and check as a class. Students can continue to work in pairs (of different fluency levels) for Exercise 2. Have students take turns asking the questions and responding with the target phrases. Monitor the pairs and remind students to use the phrases as necessary.

Expansion/Homework
To get a better feel for how these phrases are used by native speakers, students can do some research by watching an English-language program on television or listening to the radio. Help students choose a show that contains unscripted conversation (such as a panel news discussion or a talk show). Ask them to listen for ten minutes and write down the phrases of hesitation used in the conversation. Then have students report back to the class on what they heard.

 For extra listening practice, use the NorthStar Companion Video.

✪✪✪ D | SPEAKING TOPIC

Suggested Time: 50 minutes 🕐

Focus

To give students a chance to use the knowledge, vocabulary, and skills they have learned in the unit to design a high-school curriculum for immigrants.

Setup

Read through the instructions with the students. Divide students into groups of three or four (of varying language backgrounds or language levels, if possible). Have the groups do Step 1, defining the problem. If they aren't familiar with a suitable area with a large group of immigrants, suggest areas from which to choose. Then have groups do Step 2, deciding on the objectives for their school. Remind them that they will have to keep their objectives in mind while planning the class schedule in Step 3. During Step 3, encourage students to think back on classes they have taken while planning the schedule. You may want them to write down the justification for the activities they choose in order to explain them to the class in the next step. Ask the groups to look at the points for the presentation in Step 4, and have each student pick one or two points to explain to the class so everyone will have a chance to participate in the presentation. For Step 4, have each group present their plan to the class. While they are listening, the other students should take notes. After the presentations, ask students to discuss whether the objectives and daily activities were similar or different. Encourage students to question other groups if they are unsure of or disagree with anything they said.

Expansion/Homework

You can also ask students to list extracurricular activities, such as sports or counseling, that they feel would be helpful to the students.

Link to *NorthStar: Reading and Writing*

If students are also using the companion text, you can ask the groups to address how their school would deal with homesickness, nostalgia, and culture shock among the students.

✪ E | RESEARCH TOPIC

Suggested Time: 40 minutes 🕐

Focus

To give students a chance to extend the knowledge, vocabulary, and skills that they have acquired during the unit to investigate the experience of one immigrant.

Setup

Divide the class into small groups of three or four (of different language backgrounds or language levels, if possible) and ask them to come up with questions for each of the interview topics for Step 1. Write questions on the board and have students agree on which questions to ask in their interviews. Then, have students interview an immigrant. If your students are members of a particular immigrant group, encourage them to choose a person from a different group to investigate. For Step 2, have students compare what they learned from their interviews with other members of the class.

Expansion/Homework

If your students are immigrants but have interviewed people from immigrant groups other than their own, you can ask students to serve as "experts" during the discussion after the presentation, providing more information on their own group.

Link to *NorthStar: Reading and Writing*

If students are also using the companion text, you can have them incorporate the themes they studied in the readings into their research questions (e.g., weather, food, search for a better life, homesickness, and whether their new home was what they expected); see Linking Readings One and Two in *Reading and Writing*, page 204. For example, students could ask, *Was it difficult to adjust to the weather in your new home? Why?* or *How do you deal with feelings of homesickness?*

Technology:
A Blessing or a Curse?

OVERVIEW

Theme:	Technology

Listenings:	Listening One: *Noise in the City*
	    A radio news report
	Listening Two: *Technology Talk*
	    A talk radio show

Critical Thinking Skills:	Interpret cartoons Compare opinions about technology Analyze paradox in a poem Make judgments Hypothesize scenarios Draw conclusions Define a problem and propose a solution
Listening Tasks:	Infer situational context Listen for main ideas Listen for supporting details Interpret speaker's tone and word usage Take notes while listening Listen for specific information in student responses Listen for emphasis in speech Evaluate student commercials Listen to classmates' research findings and ask questions
Speaking Tasks:	Discuss opinions Make predictions Act out scripted dialogues Discuss possible future outcomes Practice gambits to express frustration Role-play a conflict between neighbors Develop and present a commercial for a gadget Present findings from research on technology
Pronunciation:	Stressed adverbial particles
Vocabulary:	Synonyms Word definitions Context clues Descriptive adjectives
Grammar:	Future perfect and future progressive

UNIT SUMMARY

This unit focuses on the ways people are annoyed and frustrated by modern technological inventions that are supposed to make life simple and more convenient. Listening One is a news report about car-alarm vigilantes in New York City who go to extreme measures to silence annoying car alarms. Listening Two contains calls to a call-in radio show from people complaining about the modern technology that frustrates them most.

The companion unit of *NorthStar: Reading and Writing* deals with contrasting views of technology in the home, from Bill Gates's computer-controlled house (built in the 1990s) to Henry David Thoreau's simple cabin (built in 1845).

1 Focus on the Topic, PAGE 205

✿✿✿ A PREDICTING

Suggested Time: 5 minutes ⏱

Focus
To get students thinking about undesirable effects of technology.

Setup
Have students work in pairs (of different language backgrounds or language levels, if possible) to look at the picture and discuss the questions. As a class, elicit answers to the questions from several of the students, trying to get a variety of opinions.

Expansion/Homework
You can also discuss these questions as a class without doing the pair work first. Try to elicit opinions from a variety of students and encourage students to discuss their answers with each other.

✿✿ B SHARING INFORMATION

Suggested Time: 20 minutes ⏱

Focus
To encourage free discussion of the positive and negative effects of modern technological inventions on our everyday life.

Setup
Have students work in pairs (of different language backgrounds, if possible) to fill in the chart. Encourage them to fill in at least one item in each box in the chart and to think of an item to add to the list. You can suggest that they add an item that they especially like or dislike. When the pairs have finished, elicit responses from the students, writing their ideas on the board. Encourage students to agree or disagree with each other by asking for responses to each idea.

Link to *NorthStar: Reading and Writing*
If students are also using the companion text, you can have them refer to the list of technological appliances in Sharing Information, page 218, in order to get ideas for more items to add to the chart.

✪✪✪C   **PREPARING TO LISTEN**

BACKGROUND
Suggested Time: 15 minutes

Focus
To explore another opinion about the impact of technology on modern life.

Setup
Have students work in small groups (of different language backgrounds, if possible), taking turns reading the excerpt from the poem and then answering the questions at the end. Then discuss the answers together as a class.

VOCABULARY FOR COMPREHENSION
Suggested Time: 15 minutes

Focus
To introduce vocabulary and concepts relating to noise pollution and law enforcement to aid listening comprehension.

Setup
Practice pronunciation of the underlined words. Then have students complete the task individually before comparing their answers with a student sitting nearby. Go over the answers as a class.

Expansion/Homework
To save time, you can assign the exercise as homework and use the class time to work on pronunciation and check answers.

2 Focus on Listening, PAGE 209

✪✪✪A   **LISTENING ONE: *Noise in the City***
Suggested Time: 10 minutes

Focus
To encourage students to make predictions about the topic of the news report.

Setup
Have students read the questions, then listen to the excerpt of the news report. Give students time to write down their answers and compare them in pairs (of different fluency levels, if possible). Then discuss the predictions with the class. Affirm each prediction as a possibility.

✪✪✪ LISTENING FOR MAIN IDEAS
Suggested Time: 15 minutes ⏱

Focus
To help students listen for the main ideas in the news report.

Setup
Have students read the statements, then mark them **T** or **F** as they listen. Play the news report once only. Allow students to compare their answers in pairs before checking them with the class.

Expansion/Homework
You can also ask the pairs to write corrections for the false statements.

✪✪✪ LISTENING FOR DETAILS
Suggested Time: 20 minutes ⏱

Focus
To help students listen for specific opinions and comments made by the people in the report.

Setup
First, have students read the questions. Play the news report again as the students take notes. Have students compare their notes with a partner; play the report again as needed so students can add to their notes. Student pairs can then write complete answers to the questions, using their notes to help them. Go over the answers as a class. If disagreements arise, replay the segments rather than simply giving the answers.

✪✪ REACTING TO THE LISTENING
Suggested Time: 20 minutes ⏱

Focus
To help students learn to distinguish between serious and humorous comments by listening to the tone of voice and word choice.

Setup
For Exercise 1, have students look at the chart. Emphasize that students should listen for what the person says as well as how he or she says it, and evaluate both aspects for their seriousness or humor. Play each excerpt, stopping the audio while students check off their choices. For Exercise 2, have students discuss the questions in small groups (of different language levels, if possible). Encourage them to give specific examples to support their opinions, and emphasize that it's possible for students to have varying opinions as long as their reasoning is sound.

Expansion/Homework
After the group discussions, you may want to lead a short discussion on why some speakers chose to use humor when discussing a serious subject, as this point may be difficult for students to discuss on their own. Replay Excerpts Two and Four for students. Explain the humorous references in the listenings, if the

students haven't picked them out already, such as when Lucille DiMaggio calls her car "innocent" (as if it were human), and when the Egg Man uses the invented word "eggworthy" (like "praiseworthy" or "trustworthy") to refer to a car whose alarm is going off. Ask students if they think these people are upset about their experiences, and if so, why they are making a joke about it.

✪✪✪B LISTENING TWO: *Technology Talk*

Suggested Time: 20 minutes 🕐

Focus

To present students with more opinions about the positive and negative aspects of modern technology.

Setup

Have students look at Exercise 1. Then play the audio as students take notes on the technology being discussed by the callers. Replay the exercise as needed. Have students check their answers in pairs (of different fluency levels, if possible). Go over the answers as a class, replaying any problematic segments instead of just giving the answer. Then have the pairs look at the cartoon in Exercise 2 and discuss the questions.

✪✪✪C LINKING LISTENINGS ONE AND TWO

Suggested Time: 30 minutes 🕐

Focus

To get students to reflect on and react to the opinions they heard about modern technology and its influence on people's lives.

Setup

Divide students into small groups (of different fluency levels, if possible) to complete the chart and discuss their ideas. Replay excerpts from both listenings as requested to help students fill in the chart.

Link to *NorthStar: Reading and Writing*

If students are also using the companion text, you can ask them to extrapolate on the possible problems that could result if the technology in Bill Gates's "Smart Home" were to malfunction as often as many car alarms do. Have students work in pairs to pick one technological advance that Bill Gates has proposed (e.g., the automatic lights; see Reading for Details, pages 224–226, in *Reading and Writing*, for a summary of the reading). Have the pairs work together to think of how the technology could malfunction and what problems it could cause. Then have them create a call to *Technology Talk*, with one student being the host and the other being the caller who is complaining about his or her Smart Home. Have the pairs perform the role plays for the class. You can also list vocabulary from both strands on the board and encourage students to use these words during their discussion.

3 Focus on Vocabulary, PAGE 215

✪ EXERCISES 1 AND 2
Suggested Time: 20 minutes ⏱

Focus
To help students understand and use the names of different sounds and adjectives to describe them.

Setup
Have students look at the list of noises in the left-hand column of the chart. They may not be familiar with most of the words, but explain that they will hear sounds on the audio that will illustrate the words for them. Play Exercise 1 as the students write in the middle column what the source of the noise probably is. After the exercise is finished, elicit the descriptions from the students, re-creating the chart on the board. For Exercise 2, have the students look at the list of adjectives; clarify any that they don't know. Students can use dictionaries if they wish. Then play the sounds again as students write down the adjectives they think best describe the sounds. Have students compare their answers with another student nearby before sharing them with the class.

Expansion/Homework
(1) To find definitions of the adjectives, you can assign one word to each student (preferably as homework the day before). Have the students look up the word in a dictionary, and warn them to read the definitions carefully so that they note down the relevant definitions only (for example, there are several definitions of *soft* that have nothing to do with sound). In class, have each student present the definition of his or her word to the class. (2) To check understanding of the vocabulary individually, you can ask students to write a short paragraph about three sounds they hear in their home and how the sounds make them feel. Collect the paragraphs, and correct the vocabulary usage. Alternatively, you could have students record their paragraphs, and you can record your feedback.

✪ EXERCISE 3
Suggested Time: 20 minutes ⏱

Focus
To deepen the students' understanding of vocabulary from the unit by completing dialogues.

Setup
Have students work in pairs (of different fluency levels, if possible) to do the exercise. Have Student A look at page 216 while Student B looks at page 228. Before starting the dialogue, give the students some time to look at the vocabulary list and complete their part of the dialogue by filling in the blanks. Then have pairs read their part of the dialogue and correct each other's answers.

Expansion/Homework

(1) Before the pairs read the dialogues, you can have **A** students pair up and **B** students pair up to compare their answers for the fill-in sections. (2) For more oral practice, you can have students improvise additional conversations using the target vocabulary. Have each student think of a type of technology they find annoying and start a dialogue complaining about it. (3) To check understanding of the vocabulary individually, you can ask students to write a dialogue using at least five of the vocabulary words for homework. Collect the dialogues, and correct the vocabulary usage. Alternatively, you could have students record the assignment.

 For extra vocabulary practice, have students work on the self-grading vocabulary activities for the unit on the NorthStar Companion Website at **http://www.longman.com/northstar**.

4 Focus on Speaking, PAGE 217

✪✪A   PRONUNCIATION: Stressed Adverbial Particles

Suggested Time: 20 minutes ⏱

Focus
To help students understand how native speakers stress adverbial particles; to give students practice stressing these particles in their own speech.

Setup
Read through the explanation together with students. Have them repeat the phrases after you to practice the stress pattern. In Exercise 1, have students listen to the recorded sentences and circle the stressed particles. Check answers as a class. For Exercise 2, have students listen to the recorded complaint, circle the stressed particles, and mark the consonant-vowel joinings. Check by having students take turns reading sentences from the excerpt. For Exercise 3, have students work in pairs (of similar fluency levels, if possible) to create a short dialogue. Have them practice the dialogue as you listen for stress and pronunciation problems. Then have students role play their dialogues for the class.

Expansion/Homework
Have students create an original role play for a different complaint.

✪✪B   GRAMMAR: Future Perfect and Future Progressive

Suggested Time: 40 minutes ⏱

Focus
To have students practice using future perfect and future progressive tenses while playing a guessing game and discussing future technological inventions. This grammatical point will also be used in the Speaking Topic, page 223.

Setup

Discover what your students know about the grammar point by having them read the examples and answer the questions in Exercise 1. Present the grammar, referring students to the grammar box on page 219. For Exercise 2, have pairs (of similar language levels, if possible) practice the future perfect. Have Student A look at page 220, while Student B looks at page 229 in the Student Activities section. First, have students look at the clues and fill in the blanks with the future perfect. Then have students take turns reading the clues one at a time while their partners guess which item is being described. Monitor the pairs to correct any verb-tense errors. For Exercise 3, have the pairs continue working together to practice the future progressive. Ask them to think about technology at the end of the next decade and to use the future progressive to describe what people will be doing then. They can discuss the items suggested in the box and also make predictions of their own. Encourage them to explain their ideas with more than one sentence. After the students finish, ask the pairs to share some of their predictions with the class. Monitor the pair work and class discussion, correcting any errors in the verb tenses.

Expansion/Homework

(1) Before reading the clues in Exercise 2, you may want two **A** students to pair up and two **B** students to pair up to check their answers for the fill-in exercise. Help the students check the verb tenses and correct any errors. (2) To check grammatical usage individually, you can ask students to complete Exercise 3 in writing for homework (after they have done the exercise in class). Then collect the papers and make corrections. (3) For further practice, offer exercises from *Focus on Grammar, High Intermediate,* and *Understanding and Using English Grammar.* See the Grammar Book References on pages 231–232 of the Student Book for specific units and chapters.

✪✪✪ C   STYLE: Expressing Frustration

Suggested Time: 30 minutes ⓟ

Focus

To help students learn to express frustration, a function that will be used again in the Speaking Topic, page 223.

Setup

With books closed, ask students to think back to the listenings and try to remember any phrases the speakers used to express their frustration with modern technology. Write the phrases students remember on the board. Then have students open their books and read the introductory statement and the phrases in the box. Have them write down phrases from the board that don't appear in the box. Divide the students into pairs (of similar fluency levels, if possible) to do the exercise. Have them read the situations one at a time and make up a role play, using the phrases on page 221 to express frustration as much as they can. Ask students to choose one role play to perform for the class.

To encourage students to use the target phrases in the role plays, ask the other students to write down the phrases expressing frustration that they hear during the role play. To give feedback to the pair that is performing, students can give their notes to the pair.

Expansion/Homework

To facilitate the exercise, you can list the vocabulary items on the board from page 216.

 For extra listening practice, use the NorthStar Companion Video.

✪✪✪D SPEAKING TOPIC

Suggested Time: 30 minutes ⏱

Focus

To give students a chance to use the knowledge, vocabulary, and skills they have learned in the unit to invent a new gadget; to have students create commercials for their gadgets.

Setup

If possible, bring in some magazines or catalogs that advertise strange or interesting gadgets. Have students discuss how these gadgets solve problems. Then, as a class or in pairs, have students brainstorm other frustrating problems. Write some of the problems on the board. In pairs, have students select one of the listed problems, or come up with a different problem to focus on. For Step 1, have students sketch their gadget and design an advertisement for it, using the guidelines in the text. Then, for Step 2, have pairs present their commercial to the class. For Step 3, have students evaluate each other's commercials. Refer to the guidelines from Step 1 to help keep critiques focused.

Expansion/Homework

(1) You can have students present their commercials in small groups, so that everyone is active at once. (2) If there are appropriate stores in your area, you can have students visit a store and explore how other gadgets are advertised. (3) You can structure the presentations to be like television advertisements. Give students a one-minute time limit in which to present their ideas. Encourage them to use costumes, sound effects, and props to make the advertisement catchy and interesting. Have students present their ads to the class. If the students have access to video equipment, they can record their ads, and then students can watch them in class or in a media lab.

Link to *NorthStar: Reading and Writing*

If students are also using the companion text, you can suggest that they think of a gadget to include in Bill Gates's Smart Home.

✪E   RESEARCH TOPIC

Suggested Time: 30 minutes

Focus
To give students a chance to use the knowledge, vocabulary, and skills that they have acquired during the unit to investigate recent developments in technology.

Setup
Have students work individually or in pairs to do the research. As a class, develop a list of questions to guide the research. (For example, *What is _____? What are the latest developments in _____? In 10/20/50 years, how will _____ be helping us in our daily lives?*) Then have students report back on their research.

Expansion/Homework
You can vary the report-back activity by having students prepare a television or radio program called "Updates in New Technology." Give each student or pair a five-minute time limit to present the technology they researched. Have the students record or videotape their presentations, structuring them as if they were part of a radio or television program. As a class, listen to or watch the reports. Have students evaluate each other's reports. Offer written feedback on content and language.

Student Book Answer Key

UNIT 1

BACKGROUND, page 3

1. F (Americans get most of their news from TV.)
2. F (Magazines and other sources are the least common.)
3. F (TV is still used more frequently than the Internet.)
4. T
5. F (Most Americans are very interested in news about crime.)
6. T
7. F (More than 50 percent think it is good.)
8. F (Most think it is good.)
9. F (They trust newspaper reporters more than they trust lawyers.)
10. F (They trust medical doctors more, but corporate executives less.)

VOCABULARY FOR COMPREHENSION, page 6

1. b	4. b	7. a	10. b
2. b	5. a	8. b	11. a
3. b	6. a	9. a	12. b
			13. b

A LISTENING ONE, page 8
Answers will vary.

LISTENING FOR MAIN IDEAS, page 8

1. a	3. b	5. c
2. b	4. c	6. b

LISTENING FOR DETAILS, page 9

1. c	3. a	5. b	7. b
2. a	4. b	6. b	8. a

REACTING TO THE LISTENING

1 page 10

Excerpt One

1. c
2. She points out that Spiegel is a medievalist whose period of study ends around 1328.

Excerpt Two

3. b
4. She says that it does seem that those involved in spiritual practices are often the most resistant to the daily news barrage.

Excerpt Three

5. a
6. They said, "I would if I could," or "Psst, don't tell anyone."

B LISTENING TWO

1 page 11

1. b	3. b	5. a	7. a
2. a	4. a	6. b	8. b

3 FOCUS ON VOCABULARY

1 page 13

1. b	4. d
2. a	5. c
3. e	

biased; to make a connection; lethal; comes in second; to take a break

6. h	9. f
7. j	10. g
8. i	

tune in; pastime; updates; riveting, soothing

2 page 15
Answers will vary.

A PRONUNCIATION

1 page 17

1. The United <u>States</u> <u>has</u> become a nation of people addicted to the news.
2. <u>Americans</u> <u>are</u> offered news in many forms
3. <u>Critics</u> <u>have</u> been concerned about the amount of news we watch.
4. Many <u>viewers</u> <u>have</u> tuned into the CornCam website.
5. <u>Academics</u> <u>are</u> worried about the amount of news we consume.

2 page 17

1. are	3. has	5. have	7. we're
2. are	4. are	6. is	8. we've

B GRAMMAR

1 page 18

1. In sentence *a,* the focus is *your mind.* In sentence *b,* the focus is *the website.* In sentence *c,* the focus is *children.*
2. *Answers will vary.*

2 page 18

2. were provided	9. have been counted
3. were flooded	10. is being planned
4. have been treated	11. will be followed
5. is being reported	12. was rescued
6. is predicted	13. had been warned
7. be regarded	14. was interviewed
8. was released	15. be given

1. was attracted
2. to be filled
3. is stimulated
4. have been depressed
5. is being promoted
6. has been visited
7. were reminded
8. was delayed

UNIT 2

VOCABULARY FOR COMPREHENSION, page 27

1. revelation
2. landscape
3. soared
4. crushed
5. collapsed
6. mangled
7. limitations
8. scars
9. crutches
10. perseverance
11. overcome
12. compassion
13. proof
14. had in store for

A   LISTENING ONE, page 28

Suggested answer:

1. The station chose essays by people who overcame obstacles to make their dreams come true.

2. *Answers will vary.*

LISTENING FOR MAIN IDEAS, page 29

1. He dreamed he was flying, though never over the same landscape.

2. He was hit by a runaway truck.

3. He realized that everyone is born with gifts, but we all run into obstacles.

4. He has learned that if we use our gifts, we can overcome our obstacles.

LISTENING FOR DETAILS, page 29

1. F (He dreamed he was flying.)
2. F (He always dreamed about different landscapes.)
3. F (He was four.)
4. F (He used crutches.)
5. F (He was in Venice.)
6. F (He was overlooking San Marco square.)
7. T
8. F (He dreamed he was flying across Italy toward the sea.)

REACTING TO THE LISTENING

1 **page 30**

Excerpt One

1. up in the air, soar. These words mean fly, especially high up in the sky.

2. crushed. In this sentence, *crushed* means defeated by someone or something.

3. *Answers will vary.*

Excerpt Two

4. . . . I couldn't fly. I could hardly walk . . .

5. *Answers will vary.*

Excerpt Three

6. I knew . . . And I also knew . . . But I knew . . .

7. *Answers will vary.*

Excerpt Four

8. a. on the rooftop
   b. up on a ledge
   c. to the left
   d. below me

9. *Answers will vary.*

B   LISTENING TWO

1 **page 32**

1. There were seven climbers.

2. Five were blind. One was deaf and asthmatic. Another was a cancer survivor and an amputee.

3. They were the largest group of disabled athletes ever to climb Mount Kilimanjaro.

4. They turned to each other for inspiration.

C   LINKING LISTENINGS ONE AND TWO, page 32

Suggested answers:

Richard Van Ornum	Achilles Track Club
1. He was hit by a truck as a child and his leg was badly hurt. He had to learn to walk again.	Different climbers had different obstacles: There were blind climbers, a deaf and asthmatic climber, a cancer survivor/amputee.
2. He wanted to walk again and generally succeed in life. He had pain from the crutches he used.	They wanted to climb Mount Kilimanjaro. Their disabilities would make the climb more difficult.
3. His imagination and perseverence helped him to achieve his goals. He believed that we all run into obstacles, but if we recognize our talents and make the best if them, we can succeed.	They had a lot of perseverance. They inspired each other.
4. He saw himself as proof that any obstacle could be overcome.	They felt that behind the personal physical challenge, there was a greater message.

3 FOCUS ON VOCABULARY

1 page 33

1. challenging	12. judging
2. determined	13. limitations
3. inspiration	14. courageous
4. landscape	15. empowerment
5. scattered	16. peak
6. swooping	17. proof
7. collapsed	18. tough
8. recognize	19. had in store for
9. inspirational	20. altitude
10. recognition	21. soaring
11. perseverance	

2 page 35

1. a. F b. L
2. a. L b. F
3. a. F b. L
4. a. L b. F
5. a. L b. F

A PRONUNCIATION

1 page 37

1. When Richard was little, he dreamed he was flying.

2. He looked at his scar and imagined it was an eagle.

3. When he visited Venice, he realized that he had great gifts.

4. He suddenly realized that he could overcome his obstacles.

5. The essay he wrote about his experience was chosen for broadcast.

2 page 37

- Richard's scar looked like an eagle that was flying on his leg.

- A runaway truck hit Richard Van Ornum and he couldn't walk after the accident.

- Richard's leg was mangled when he was on a field trip in preschool.

- The Achilles Track Club is the organization that decided to undertake this remarkable project.

- The athletes who participated in the climb talked emotionally about their achievement.

- Many newspapers showed photos of the athletes as they climbed the mountain.

B GRAMMAR

1 page 38

1. The underlined words are gerunds.

2. The underlined words are infinitives.

C STYLE

1 page 42

Members of the Achilles Track <u>Club</u>, an <u>organization</u> for people with disabilities, have just managed to climb Kilimanjaro, one of the highest mountain peaks in the world. On their backs they carried their equipment, but in their hearts they also carried the hopes and dreams of everyone who at some point in their lives has felt <u>afraid</u>, <u>fearful</u>, or <u>intimidated</u>. As they reached the summit, with the mist below them, the peaks all around them, and the sun above them, their hearts were full of pride and joy. They showed us the truth in the words of American writer Ralph Waldo Emerson: "What lies behind us and what lies before us are tiny matters compared to what lies within us."

UNIT 3

BACKGROUND

1 page 47

1. e	4. a
2. c	5. b
3. d	

VOCABULARY FOR COMPREHENSION, page 48

a. 11	d. 13	g. 3	j. 7
b. 12	e. 1	h. 2	k. 8
c. 9	f. 4	i. 5	l. 10
			m. 6

A LISTENING ONE, page 50

1. b	3. *Answers will vary.*
2. b	4. *Answers will vary.*

LISTENING FOR MAIN IDEAS, page 50

1. Teenagers are "night owls" because they have a lot to do. Also, melatonin keeps them awake.

2. They get sleepy at school and are unable to stay fully awake throughout the school day.

3. They can face danger if they are riding a bike, playing sports, using tools, or driving.

4. They can get frustrated, irritable, and sad.

LISTENING FOR DETAILS, page 51

1. b	4. b	7. c
2. a	5. b	8. b
3. a	6. b	9. c

REACTING TO THE LISTENING

1 page 52

Excerpt One

1. playful, amused
2. elongated word length, changes in tone

Excerpt Two

3. enthusiastic, respectful
4. exaggerated word stress

Excerpt Three

5. confused, unhappy
6. changes in intonation, elongated word length, exaggerated word stress

Excerpt Four

7. shocked
8. exaggerated word stress

B LISTENING TWO, page 54

1. b   3. b   5. b   7. b
2. a   4. b   6. a

C LINKING LISTENINGS ONE AND TWO, page 55

Questions about the Listenings

What are some of the *causes* of sleep deprivations?
Listening One: Teenagers have a biological need to go to sleep late. Their school schedule starts early, so they are constantly tired.
Listening Two: Parents of young children can't get the sleep they need. The children sleep a little and wake up a lot. Parents don't make sleep a priority, and sleep loss accumulates.

What are some of the *symptoms* of not getting enough sleep?
Listening One: Teenagers feel miserable. They fall asleep in school. When tired, teens are more easily frustrated, more irritable, more prone to sadness. Their performance on intellectual tasks drops.
Listening Two: People get tired and cranky.

What are some of the *dangers* of sleep deprivation?
Listening One: Reaction time, alertness, and concentration are all slowed down by insufficient sleep. The Federal Department of Transportation estimates teenage drivers cause more than half of all fall-asleep crashes.
Listening Two: Their job performance is affected. Parents make bad decisions. Parents are too tired to exercise. Parents feel they may not be safe drivers when they are tired.

What *recommendations* did the doctors and researchers make about our sleep habits?
Listening One: Teenagers, parents, and school authorities need to know more about the science of sleep and how important it is to young people's health.
Listening Two: We need to make sleep a priority.

3 FOCUS ON VOCABULARY

1 page 58

a. 1	e. 2	i. 8	m. 14
b. 10	f. 7	j. 11	n. 15
c. 3	g. 5	k. 13	o. 6
d. 4	h. 12	l. 9	

A PRONUNCIATION

1 page 58

1. I <u>need</u> to go to <u>bed</u>, but I'm <u>feeling</u> <u>energetic</u>.
2. <u>Adolescents</u> wake up <u>late</u>, but <u>children</u> wake up <u>early</u>.
3. <u>Lian</u> is fast <u>asleep</u>, but her <u>children</u> are <u>awake</u>.
4. My <u>husband</u> has <u>insomnia</u>, but <u>I</u> need to <u>sleep</u>.
5. I'm <u>sleepy</u> in the <u>morning</u>, but I'm wide <u>awake</u> at <u>night</u>.

B GRAMMAR

1 page 60

1. The doctor suggests going to bed earlier and taking naps.
2. The woman doesn't go to bed early or take naps.
3. *Answers will vary.*

2 page 61

2. wouldn't get		11. fell	
3. would you do		12. took	
4. slept		13. would be	
5. showed up		14. didn't get	
6. worked		15. would be	
7. would be		16. would happen	
8. weren't allowed		17. didn't sleep	
9. would be		18. would increase	
10. would happen		19. didn't institute	

UNIT 4

BACKGROUND, page 70

1. d   4. f
2. e   5. c
3. b   6. a

VOCABULARY FOR COMPREHENSION, page 72

a. 7	e. 2	i. 13	m. 9
b. 5	f. 3	j. 8	n. 10
c. 4	g. 6	k. 15	o. 11
d. 1	h. 12	l. 14	

A LISTENING ONE, page 73

1. . . . the beaches to be packed with tourists . . .
2. . . . eerily silent
3. . . . are hard to find

4. . . . the checkout counter

5. . . . getting ready for a hurricane

LISTENING FOR MAIN IDEAS, page 74

<u>8</u> a resident who almost lost her house

<u>3</u> a resident who is not evacuating

<u>6</u> a tourist who is scared

<u>7</u> advice for tourists

<u>4</u> how hurricane forecasts are made

<u>5</u> supplies that people should buy

<u>1</u> the mood in Homestead, Florida

<u>2</u> the weather report

LISTENING FOR DETAILS, page 75

1. c	4. c	7. c	10. b
2. a	5. b	8. a	11. a
3. c	6. a	9. b	12. c

REACTING TO THE LISTENING

1 page 76

Excerpt One

1. overconfident
2. He laughs in a sarcastic way. He sounds dismissive.

Excerpt Two

3. guarded
4. He sounds serious.

Excerpt Three

5. fearful
6. She laughs nervously.

Excerpt Four

7. confident
8. She laughs.

B LISTENING TWO, page 77

1. The Hurricane Hunters fly into the eye of the storm to gather information and relay it back to the mainland.

2. There are rough winds outside the hurricane, but once inside the eye, the weather is calm and peaceful.

3. By providing an eyewitness account and looking down at the surface of the water, humans can tell certain things about the speed and direction of the storm that computers cannot.

4. They say the experience is intense and heartening because it helps save people's lives.

C LINKING LISTENINGS ONE AND TWO

1 page 78

Possible answers:

Hurricane Hunters	Local Authorities (Mayor, Police, Firefighters)
How will you communicate with the public about the hurricane?	When will the hurricane get here?
Do people know how to get supplies?	How strong will it be?
Have you set up a place for people to go if their homes are damaged?	How long will it last?

3 FOCUS ON VOCABULARY

1 page 79

1. a. exciting
   b. excited
2. a. amazed
   b. amazing
3. a. interesting
   b. interested
4. a. frightened
   b. frightening
5. a. heartening
   b. heartened
6. a. comforting
   b. comforted
7. a. encouraging
   b. encouraged
8. a. surprising
   b. surprised

A PRONUNCIATION

1 page 82

1. People are buying batteries, water bottles, and flashlights.

2. The sky is blue, the ocean is calm, and the beaches are empty.

3. My house was flooded, my furniture was ruined, and my car is gone.

4. The hurricane has passed by Cuba, Puerto Rico, and southern Florida.

5. There were big hurricanes in 1938, 1965, and 1997.

B GRAMMAR

1 page 83

1. In sentence a, *that* refers to the noun *information.* In sentence b, *which* refers to the noun *eye wall.*

2. The information added to the sentences after the underlined words describes the nouns. The information acts as an adjective.

2 page 85

2. which	11. that	19. which
3. where	12. where	20. which
4. whose	13. that	21. that
5. that	14. whose	22. whose
6. when	15. when	23. who
7. whose	16. who	24. when
8. who	17. who	25. which
9. when	18. that	26. which
10. who		

UNIT 5

B SHARING INFORMATION

1 page 92

1. b   4. a
2. d   5. c
3. e

VOCABULARY FOR COMPREHENSION, page 94

1. j   5. a   9. c
2. f   6. h   10. g
3. e   7. i
4. d   8. b

A LISTENING ONE, PAGE 95

1. The Great Life is the one spirit that fills all things—humans, plants, rocks. The sum of all of that and more is what we call the Great Life.

2. *Answers will vary.*

LISTENING FOR MAIN IDEAS, page 96

1. First Law of Nature: You don't take anything without a reason. Example: for food, for medicine, or for protection.

2. Second Law of Nature: Everything we do should serve the Great Life. Example: It's better to use a manual toothbrush rather than an electric one.

3. Third Law of Nature: Don't pollute where we live. Example: Don't pour chemical wastes down the drain.

LISTENING FOR DETAILS, page 96

1. b   6. b
2. b   7. a
3. c   8. c
4. c   9. a
5. a

B LISTENING TWO

1 page 98

1. disagree
2. agree
3. disagree
4. agree
5. agree

2 page 98

1. disagree
2. agree
3. disagree
4. agree
5. agree
6. agree

3 page 99

You cannot understand this land with <u>maps</u>,

lines drawn as if earth were an <u>animal's</u> carcass

cut into pieces, skinned,

though always <u>less eaten</u> than thrown away.

<u>See</u> this land instead with a wind-eagle's eyes,

linked with <u>rivers</u> and <u>streams</u> like sinews through leather,

sewed strong to hold the <u>people</u> to the <u>earth</u>.

Do not try to know the land by <u>roads</u>.

Let your <u>feet</u> instead caress the soil in the way of deer,

whose trails <u>follow</u> the ways of least resistance.

When you feel this land

when you <u>taste</u> this land

when you hold this land as lungs hold breath

when your songs <u>see</u> this land,

when your ears sing this land,

<u>You will be</u> this land.

<u>You will be</u> this land.

3 FOCUS ON VOCABULARY

1 page 100

Noun	Verb	Adjective	Adverb
1. benefit	benefit	beneficial	beneficially
2. competition	compete	competitive	competitively
3. electricity	electrocute, electrify	electric, electrical	electrically
4. industry, industrialization	industrialize	industrial, industrialized	x
5. nature	x	natural	naturally
6. pollution	pollute	polluted	x
7. protection	protect	protected, protective	protectively
8. recycling	recycle	recycled	x
9. spirit	x	spiritual	spiritually
10. waste	waste	wasteful	wastefully

2 **page 101**

1. **a.** benefit, **b.** beneficial, **c.** benefit
2. **a.** competitive, **b.** compete, **c.** competition
3. **a.** electricity, **b.** electrify, **c.** electrically, **d.** electrical
4. **a.** industrialization, **b.** industrial, **c.** industrialize
5. **a.** nature, **b.** natural, **c.** naturally
6. **a.** pollute, **b.** polluted, **c.** pollution
7. **a.** protect, **b.** protective, **c.** protection
8. **a.** recycling, **b.** recycle, **c.** recycled
9. **a.** spiritually, **b.** spiritual, **c.** spirits
10. **a.** wastefully, **b.** wasteful, **c.** waste

A PRONUNCIATION

1 **page 104**

1. three	5. so	9. sued	13. breeze
2. they	6. ladder	10. day	14. Zen
3. there	7. worthy	11. bathe	
4. think	8. dough	12. other	

B GRAMMAR

1 **page 105**

1. The paragraph is about actions in the past.
2. All of the sentences focus on things that were not done.
3. The paragraph communicates the feeling that some things should have been done differently, but weren't.

2 **page 107**

1. couldn't have known
2. shouldn't have poured
3. shouldn't have built
4. ought to have been
5. could have stayed
6. shouldn't have happened

UNIT 6

BACKGROUND, page 114
Suggested answers:

a. 1, 5, 13
b. 4, 8
c. 4, 8

VOCABULARY FOR COMPREHENSION, page 117

a. 10	d. 9	g. 3	j. 6
b. 12	e. 5	h. 7	k. 4
c. 2	f. 8	i. 11	l. 1

A LISTENING ONE, page 118
Possible answers:

1. She did something important with the money she saved.
2. *Answers will vary.*

LISTENING FOR MAIN IDEAS, page 118

1. T
2. F (She saved $250,000.)
3. T
4. T
5. F (She did not regret giving her money away. She wished she had more to give.)
6. T

LISTENING FOR DETAILS, page 119

1. c	4. c	7. b	9. c
2. c	5. b	8. b	10. a
3. b	6. a		

REACTING TO THE LISTENING

1 **page 120**
Possible answers:

Excerpt One

1. Reasons: help people who can't afford to go to college, help people do something she couldn't do

Excerpt Two

2. Reasons: change society, help people do something she couldn't do

Excerpt Three

3. Reasons: show that giving is important

B LISTENING TWO

1 **page 121**

	What Is the Announcement Asking People to Do?	According to the Announcement, Why Should People Do It?
PSA 1	Volunteer time and money	Not because we have to, but because we should, and many Americans do
PSA 2	Volunteer our services such as driving for people who can't	This will make us feel something real

C LINKING LISTENINGS ONE AND TWO, page 122
Answers will vary.

3 FOCUS ON VOCABULARY

1 **page 122**

1. recipient	7. stunned
2. retired	8. touched
3. volunteer	9. fund
4. tucked away	10. regretted
5. nest egg	11. benefactor
6. donation	

A PRONUNCIATION

1 page 126

1. Q Oseola McCarty saved her money for about 50 years, didn't she?

2. C Wealthy philanthropists save a lot of money on taxes, don't they?

3. C A lot of Americans donate to charity, don't they?

4. Q People give more today than they used to, don't they?

5. C Children in your country are encouraged to volunteer, aren't they?

2 page 126

Mr. Generous: That's a good idea. Let's see . . . I admire the work of the Dinosaur Egg Association, don't you? They're trying to find out how to re-create dinosaurs from ancient DNA samples.

Mrs. Generous: Well, that's interesting, yes, but I'm more impressed by Save the Rain Forests, or the Clean Ocean Fund. It helps clean up the oceans. I think we should encourage more ecological programs, don't you?

Mr. Generous: Well, I guess so. Look at this one! How about the Space Alien Research Institute? It would be great to make contact with some aliens from outer space, wouldn't it?

Mrs. Generous: Now that's silly, isn't it? Here's something serious. How about Options for Independence? It's an organization that helps elderly people live on their own. I think that's important, don't you?

B GRAMMAR

1 page 127

1. The underlined phrases are similar because they are questions.

2. The underlined phrases are different because *did you* is affirmative and *isn't it* is negative.

2 page 128

Steps 1 and 2

1. haven't you?
2. isn't it?
3. aren't they?
4. would they?
5. do they?
6. isn't it?
7. didn't he?
8. isn't it?
9. shouldn't they?

3 page 129

Step 1

2. After finishing high school (She didn't finish high school.)

3. She was careful about watching her nest egg as it grew. (She was surprised to learn how much money she had saved.)

4. When her three children grew up and moved away (She had no children.)

5. . . . college professors (She decided to help promising black students.)

6. . . . $100,000 (She donated most of her life savings— $250,000.)

7. . . . didn't accept the money because she felt sorry for Oseola (She accepted the money gratefully.)

8. Oseola couldn't afford to stop working (Oseola no longer washes clothes for a living.)

UNIT 7

VOCABULARY FOR COMPREHENSION, page 137

1. b
2. a
3. a
4. c
5. a
6. b
7. c
8. a
9. a
10. c
11. c
12. a

A LISTENING ONE, page 139

1. b
2. *Answers will vary.*

LISTENING FOR MAIN IDEAS, page 139
Suggested answers:

What is the person's job?

Betty Cortina: Elementary school teacher
Jim McDonald: Management training executive

Can EQ be learned or taught?

Betty Cortina: Thinks EQ skills can be learned and should be taught.
Jim McDonald: Thinks it is difficult for adults to learn EQ skills, although it might be possible for children.

How can a high EQ help a person?

Betty Cortina: Thinks high EQ can help children overcome their frustrations and get along with their peers.
Jim McDonald: Thinks high EQ helps people work with others.

LISTENING FOR DETAILS, page 140

1, 3, 5, 6, 8, 10, 12, 13, 14

REACTING TO THE LISTENING

1 **page 141**
Possible answers:

Excerpt One

1. Skills needed: self-awareness, self-control, people skills

2. Reason: To improve the following: responding to pressure, handling stress, and interacting with other people.

Excerpt Two

3. Skills needed: self-awareness, self-control

4. Reason: The child needs to deal with her frustration so she can do better in school.

Excerpt Three

5. Skills needed: self-awareness, self-control, self-motivation, people skills

6. Reason: Managers need to respond well to whatever is going on around them. They shouldn't get angry and resentful when there is a problem.

B LISTENING TWO

2 **page 142**
High EQ answers:

1. b	3. c	5. b
2. a	4. c	

3 FOCUS ON VOCABULARY

1 **page 144**

1. a. enthusiastic (about)
   b. respond well
2. a. high-spirited
   b. deal with setbacks
3. a. make a fuss
   b. put aside our negative feelings
4. a. put myself in my client's shoes
   b. perceptive
5. a. swallow your pride
   b. take life in stride

A PRONUNCIATION

1 **page 147**

2. ad | just
3. suc | cess
4. pro | duc | tive | ly
5. peo | ple
6. ho | nest
7. quo | tient
8. re | sent | ful
9. per | son | al
10. a | bi | li | ty
11. a | dult
12. per | cep | tive
13. fai | lure
14. ad | vice
15. e | mo | tion | al

3 **page 147**

Emotional Intelligence Seminar

Self-Awareness
Understanding yourself

Self-Control
Handling emotions

Self-Motivation
Using emotions productively

Empathy
Understanding others' emotions

People Skills
Relating well to people

Led by psychologist Nancy Matz

B GRAMMAR

1 **page 148**

1. In sentence *a*, the speaker's exact words were, "Some kids tend to be much more patient than others." In sentence *b*, the speaker's exact words were, "We could learn to improve our EQ."

2. In sentence *a*, the second verb is in the past tense because the speaker is using indirect (reported) speech.

3. Sentence *b* uses the simple past tense and the modal *could* + base form of the verb.

UNIT 8

VOCABULARY FOR COMPREHENSION

1 **page 157**
Answers will vary.

2 **page 159**

1. c	4. k	7. b	10. h
2. j	5. d	8. g	11. a
3. i	6. e	9. f	

A LISTENING ONE, page 159

1. Eating habits are changing.

2. Answers will vary, but students may mention busy lifestyles, easy availability of fast food and prepared food.

LISTENING FOR MAIN IDEAS, page 160

1. take-out sandwiches

2. changes in the workforce; more women working; more men with white-collar jobs than before; less time for midday meal; eating less food for lunch

3. The bakery now offers take-out sandwiches.

1. b	4. a	7. c
2. c	5. a	8. b
3. b	6. b	9. b
		10. b

REACTING TO THE LISTENING

1 page 161

Excerpt One

1. b   2. a

Excerpt Two

3. b   4. b

Excerpt Three

5. b   6. b

Excerpt Four

7. a   8. b

B   LISTENING TWO, page 162

1. a	3. b	5. a	7. a
2. a	4. b	6. b	

C   LINKING LISTENINGS ONE AND TWO, page 163

Conversation One

Speaker A: Claude Fishlere / analytical
Speaker B: Satellite Sister / light, informal

Conversation 2

Speaker A: Satellite Sister / light, informal
Speaker B: Bakery, owner / informative, analytical

Conversation 3

Speaker A: Satellite Sister / light, informal
Speaker B: Bakery owner / informative

Conversation 4

Speaker A: Claude Fishlere / analytical
Speaker B: Bakery owner / informative, analytical

3   FOCUS ON VOCABULARY

2 page 166

a. 7	d. 10	g. 5	i. 4
b. 6	e. 3	h. 9	j. 1
c. 2	f. 8		

A   PRONUNCIATION

1 page 168

1. lock	4. boot
2. wool	5. boost
3. body	6. cook

2 page 169

/uw/ **too**	/ʊ/ **good**	Other (not /uw/ or /ʊ/)
too	book	flood
boom	cook	blood
noodles	look	
noon	tool	
cool		

3 page 169

/ɑ/ **not**	/ow/ **no**	/ə/ **Monday**	Other (not /ɑ/, /ow/, or /ə/)
shock	home	oven	women
possible	whole	done	do
job	frozen	money	
	explode	come	
	go		

B   GRAMMAR

1 page 170

1. *Answers will vary.*

2. In sentence *a*, *it* refers to *lunch.* In sentence *d*, *them* refers to *children.*

2 page 172

1. call you up	9. thinking it over
2. caught on	10. hand it in
3. check it out	11. work it out
4. ask you over	12. call me back
5. turn him down	13. turned it on
6. put him off	14. try it out
7. call it off	15. run into them
8. letting you down	

3 page 174

2. f	6. b	10. n	14. i
3. a	7. g	11. o	15. h
4. d	8. l	12. j	
5. e	9. m	13. k	

UNIT 9

BACKGROUND

1 page 180

i. China	j. Korea
b. Columbia	f. Nigeria
c. the Dominican Republic	e. Poland
h. Egypt	g. Russia
	d. West Indies

VOCABULARY FOR COMPREHENSION

2 page 183

1. g	4. l	7. d	10. c
2. k	5. e	8. h	11. f
3. b	6. j	9. a	12. i

A LISTENING ONE, page 184

Possible answers:

1. The International High School is successful because students use both their native language and their new language, English. Students feel confident in their native language, so they are better able to learn in general, including in their new language.

2. Students in other high school programs probably use one language at a time.

LISTENING FOR MAIN IDEAS, page 184

1, 2, 4, 5, 6, 8 *(Item 8 is inferred.)*

LISTENING FOR DETAILS, page 185

Suggested answers:

Jennifer Shenke: Teacher. She likes the fact that students enjoy themselves, help each other, and learn at the same time.

Priscilla Billarrel: Student. She feels that the students understand, support, and correct each other without making fun of each other's mistakes.

Aaron Listhaus: Teacher. He thinks it is important that school is a "safe" place where students feel welcomed and valued for who they are.

Evelyna Namovich: Student. She was not punished for speaking Polish and she was encouraged to bone up on Polish while she was learning English.

Kathy Rucker: Teacher. She feels that speaking another language has a practical economic value because there's so much rapid travel and international business.

REACTING TO THE LISTENING

1 page 185

Excerpt One

1. b   2. *and*; laughter

Excerpt Two

3. c   4. *home; problem*

Excerpt Three

5. a   6. *travel; business*

B LISTENING TWO

1 page 187

1. a	3. b	5. c	7. b
2. c	4. a	6. a	8. a

2 page 188

1. foreign	6. jokes
2. breath	7. escape
3. words	8. tongue
4. order	9. book
5. miss	10. thinking

3 FOCUS ON VOCABULARY

1 page 190

1. uprooted	9. extended
2. blend in	10. tight-knit
3. intimidated	11. suppressed
4. encourage	12. deal with
5. support	13. adaptation
6. set him apart	14. challenged
7. interpret	15. relieved
8. value	16. niche

A PRONUNCIATION

1 page 194

She: international, traditional, punishment, special, communication, niche, flourish

Pleasure: measure, usual, television, occasion, treasure

Child: lecture, culture, Chile, niche

Just: language, enjoy, adjust, subject, educators, encourage

B GRAMMAR

1 page 196

1. Sentence *a* is about actions in the present.

2. Sentence *b* is about actions in the past.

3. Sentence *c* focuses on activities that are continuing in the present.

2 page 198

1. came	19. isn't
2. was	20. are
3. didn't speak	21. have changed
4. went	22. is
5. weren't	23. look
6. had	24. have spoken
7. was	25. attend
8. didn't understand	26. are learning
9. was talking *or* talked	27. love
10. asked	28. are becoming *or* have become
11. became	
12. told	29. teach *or* are teaching
13. wanted	30. help *or* are helping
14. felt	31. teach *or* are teaching
15. thought	32. hasn't spoken
16. felt	33. doesn't remember
17. doesn't speak	34. wishes
18. has changed	35. has been taking

3 page 200

Student A

1. How long has she been in the United States?
2. How did she feel about speaking Chinese when she was a girl in school in the United States?
3. How does she feel about it now?
4. Why have her feelings changed?
5. What new technology is changing the way people learn other languages?
6. How do you feel when people speak a language you don't understand?

Student B

7. What is Dr. Chin's native language?
8. What are the benefits of a bilingual school?
9. How has the bilingual school helped Dr. Chin's children?
10. What types of jobs require a bilingual person?
11. How do Dr. Chin's views about language differ from her grandparents' views?
12. In your opinion, what kind of school is best for immigrant children?

C STYLE

2 page 202

Student A	Student B
1. Germany	5. no
2. no	6. Mexico
3. from 1820–1975	7. no
4. no	8. about 350,000

UNIT 10

VOCABULARY FOR COMPREHENSION, page 208

1. c	5. b	9. a	13. a
2. c	6. c	10. c	14. a
3. a	7. a	11. a	15. b
4. a	8. a	12. a	

A LISTENING ONE, page 209
Possible answers:

1. A car alarm could be causing the noise.
2. People are annoyed and upset when they hear it.
3. *Answers will vary.*
4. The report takes place in a big, noisy city.

LISTENING FOR MAIN IDEAS, page 210

1. F	3. F	5. F
2. T	4. T	6. T

LISTENING FOR DETAILS, page 210
Suggested answers:

1. a. People are awakened often and don't know if they'll be reawakened.
   b. People are arrested for disturbing the peace.
2. a. They send the driver a note or break an egg on the windshield.
   b. Other groups smear axle grease on door handles and Vaseline on the windshield. Some break windshields.
3. a. Her car was dented.
   b. When she set her alarm off in the restaurant parking lot, nobody bothered to see if her car was being broken into.
4. a. Another night, a car was being mutilated. She called the police, and they came 40 minutes later.
   b. Car alarms should be banned in densely populated neighborhoods.
5. a. The noise affects people's ability to sleep at night and their ability to work during the day.
   b. More and more studies show that young people in particular develop hearing loss from loud noise.
6. a. The laws are now being enforced. It is now illegal for alarms to run more than three minutes. After that, the police can break into a car to disable the alarm or even tow away the car.
   b. If car owners adjusted their alarms to be less sensitive, the alarms would not be set off by vibrations from passing trucks and the like.

REACTING TO THE LISTENING

1 page 211
Answers may vary.

	Mostly Serious	Somewhat Serious	Somewhat Humorous	Mostly Humorous
Excerpt One: Judy Evans				
Tone of voice		✓		
Choice of words		✓		
Excerpt Two: Lucille DeMaggio				
Tone of voice	✓			
Choice of words	✓			
Excerpt Three: Senator Abate				
Tone of voice	✓			
Choice of words	✓			
Excerpt Four: "Egg man"				
Tone of voice				✓
Choice of words				✓

B LISTENING TWO

1 page 212

Caller 1

Technology: Stanley complains about automated phone systems.
Reason it drives the caller crazy: They drive him crazy because they take so long.

Caller 2

Technology: Carol is complaining about cellular phones.
Reason the caller finds it frustrating: People use them in public places, and this disturbs others.

Caller 3

Technology: Jessica complains about all the remote controls in her house.
Reason the caller is frustrated: They are so complicated to use, and they get lost.

Caller 4

Technology: Arthur complains about e-mail.
Reason it drives the caller crazy: It's mostly junk, and it takes too long to read.

2 page 213

A "midlife crisis" is a time in people's lives, usually between 35 and 55, when they question the meaning or usefulness of their lives and perhaps want to make a big change. The message of the cartoon is that technology, like people, gets older and may become less useful. Technology needs to change with the times.

3 FOCUS ON VOCABULARY

1 page 215
Possible answers:

Noise	What Probably Makes This Noise	Adjectives to describe the noise
1. Bang	Door or window closing	Answers will vary
2. Shatter	Glass breaking	
3. Ring	Telephone	
4. Rattle	Train wheels	
5. Beep	Microwave oven	
6. Creak	Door	
7. Whistle	Tea kettle	
8. Tick	Clock	
9. Screech	Car stopping short	
10. Honk	Car horn	

A PRONUNCIATION

1 page 217

1. I tried to read the instructions, but then I gave up.
2. I asked him to turn it down, but he said he didn't want to.
3. Come in and sit down. You really look worn out.
4. I want to buy a new car. This one keeps breaking down.
5. I'm taking this new gadget back. I can't get it to work, and I'm really fed up.

2 page 218

I give up. I've had it with these modern appliances! I bought a new alarm clock, but it goes off whenever it feels like it. Last night it went off at midnight. I got up before I realized what time it was. First I got angry and threw it out. Then I took it out of the garbage and decided to take it back. I want to get my money back.

3 page 218

1. e	3. c	5. d
2. a	4. b	

B GRAMMAR

1 page 218

1. The sentences are about activities in the future.
2. In sentence *a*, the action will already have been completed by a certain time in the future. The verbs in the sentences show the relationship between two future events. In sentence *b*, the actions will be in progress at a specific time in the future.

1 page 220

Mystery Item 1

1. will have replaced
2. will have been made

Mystery Item 2

1. will have used
2. will have used

Mystery Item 3

1. will have turned on
2. won't have become

Mystery Item 4

1. will have asked
2. will have been invented

Mystery Item 5

1. will have had
2. will have introduced

Mystery Item 6

1. will have been turned on
2. will have switched

Unit Word List

The **Unit Word List** is a summary of key vocabulary from the Student Book's Vocabulary for Comprehension and Focus on Vocabulary sections. The words are presented by unit, in alphabetical order.

Unit 1

advice
antagonism
appeal to
be addicted to
be plugged into
bias
biased
come in second
despair (noun)
disengage from
get perspective on
have a lock on
immobilize
immobilized
inconsequential
intake (noun)

lethal
make a connection
newsworthy
odds are
pastime
regardless of
remedy (noun)
repetitive
riveting
sense of humor
soothing
take a break
tune in
unappealing
underlying
update (noun)

Unit 2

altitude
challenging
collapse
collapsed
compassion
courageous
crush
crutches
determined
empowerment
get to the top
have something in store
    for someone
inspiration
inspirational
judge (verb)
landscape
limitation

make it
mangle
overcome (verb)
peak (noun)
perseverance
proof
reach a high point
reach deep down
recognition
recognize
revelation
scar (noun)
scattered
soar
soaring
swooping
tough
turn around

Unit 3

accumulate
alert (adjective)
alertness
be out of sync with
blink (verb)
captivated
chronic lack of sleep
chronically
cranky
dim (adjective)
do without
droop
fatigue

hormone
irritable
miserable
priority
secrete
sleep deprived
snore
spontaneous
subtle
surge (noun)
suspect (verb)
wave of sleepiness

Unit 4

amazed
amazing
atmospheric conditions
caught off guard
coast (noun)
comforted
comforting
contaminated
deceptively
dislocated
encouraged
encouraging
evacuate
excited
exciting
eye of the storm
eye wall
flooded
forecast (verb)
foul
frightened
frightening
heartened

heartening
inland
intensity
interested
interesting
jittery
manual (adjective)
object (noun)
outage
panic (verb)
provisions
route (noun)
scared stiff
second-guess (verb)
sophisticated
spiral rain bands
stock up (on)
storm surge
surprised
surprising
vital
vulnerable

Unit 5

beneficial
benefit (noun)
benefit (verb)
compete
compete with
competition
competitive
Earth
electrical
electrically
electricity
electrify
gather
industrial
industrialization
industrialize
manual (adjective)
manual (noun)
natural
naturally

nature
organic
pollute
polluted
pollution
protect
protection
protective
recycle
recycled
recycling
sacred
serve
spirit
spiritual
spiritually
sum
take life
waste (verb)
wind up

Unit 6

benefactor
charity
donate
donation
donor
feed the hungry
foundation
fund (verb)
laundry
nest egg
philanthropy
pledge (verb)
provide

recipient
regret (noun)
regret (verb)
retired
scholarship
show someone up
stun (verb)
stunned
touched
touch someone
tuck away
volunteer (noun)
volunteer (verb)

Unit 7

act with respect
deal with setbacks
dwell on
easygoing
empathize with
enthusiastic
give up
handle (verb)
high-spirited
make a fuss
make allowances for
patient

perceptive
put aside negative
  feelings
put oneself in someone
  else's shoes
resentful
respond
respond well
setback (noun)
sharp
swallow one's pride
take life in stride

Unit 8

A watched pot never boils.
boom (noun)
bread and butter
breadwinner
bring home the bacon
core (noun)
delicacy
demand for (noun)
dough
exploding
feminization
food for thought
franchise
get cooking
hands-free
hit (noun)
intimate (adjective)

let one's imagination run
  wild
overrun (adjective)
phenomenon
shift (noun)
sit-down (adjective)
stack (verb)
stir up trouble
take-out (adjective)
Too many cooks spoil the
  broth.
trouble brewing
utensil
white-collar (adjective)
white-collarization
witness (verb)

Unit 9

adaptation
assimilated
blend in
bone up on
challenge (noun)
challenge (verb)
deal with
encourage
extend
flourish (verb)
foreign
interpret
intimidating

mainstream
mainstream culture
native tongue
niche
relieved
set apart
support (verb)
suppress
tight-knit
unique
uproot
uprooted
value (verb)

Unit 10 _____

911
aggravating
annoying
awful
ban (verb)
banned
comforting
constant
defective
disturb the peace
drive someone crazy
faint
frazzled
get under one's skin
go off
have had it
irritated
irritating
jolt (noun)
jolt (verb)

mutilated
nagging
nasty
offense
pay a fine
piercing
posse
prompt (verb)
retaliatory
rhythmic
send someone over the
    edge
shatter
shrill
sonic
startling
tow away
vibrations
vigilante

Introduction to Achievement Tests

The following reproducible Achievement Tests allow teachers to evaluate students' progress and to identify any areas where the students might have problems in developing their listening and speaking skills. The Achievement Tests should be given upon completion of the corresponding Student Book unit.

Description   There are two Achievement Tests for each unit. **Test 1** is a "paper and pencil" test of receptive skills. It assesses students' mastery of listening comprehension and of the vocabulary, pronunciation, and grammar points introduced in the unit.

Test 2 is intended to assess the students' productive, or speaking, skills. It consists of a speaking task related to the content of the unit. Each speaking task is designed to elicit a speech sample lasting several minutes.

Administration   Administration of **Test 1** requires use of the recorded material on the audio CD packaged with this Teacher's Manual. Students will need to listen to the audio program in order to answer the questions in each section of the test. The answer key to the tests and the audioscript of the material on the CD are included at the end of the Achievement Test section.

Teachers can decide how to incorporate **Test 2** (the speaking task) into their testing situations. Some teachers will assign each speaking task immediately after students complete **Test 1**; others may decide to set aside another time to complete it. The tasks may be set up for pairs, small groups, the whole class, or on a teacher-to-student basis. When set up for pairs or small groups, teachers will need to circulate around the classroom and spend enough time with each pair or group to evaluate the production of individual students.

Some teachers may not find it possible to evaluate all of the students on every speaking test. As an alternative, teachers may choose to evaluate only part of a class on a given **Test 2** speaking task and evaluate the remaining students on tests given at a later time. Teachers may also choose to evaluate students only on every other test or on a total of three or four tests over the term.

Scoring Test 1   Individual test items are worth one point, for a maximum total of 30 points per test. To facilitate scoring, an answer key is provided at the end of the book. A student's score can be obtained by adding together the number of correct items. To obtain an overall "listening score" for a student, teachers may average all of the **Test 1** scores that the student received in the class.

Scoring Test 2   Speaking tasks are evaluated holistically using the categories in the rating sheet that follows. The categories include content, vocabulary, pronunciation, and grammar. In each category, 0 indicates poor or inadequate performance for the level; 1 indicates average or acceptable performance; 2 indicates good or outstanding performance. The teacher circles the rating for each category and adds the numbers to obtain a total score out of 8 possible points.

Test 2 Rating Sheet

Student: _____ Unit _____

Content	0	1	2
Vocabulary	0	1	2
Pronunciation	0	1	2
Grammar	0	1	2

Total Score _____

The teacher can complete the rating sheet for each student's test and give it to the student. It can also be kept by the teacher as a record of each student's progress.

An overall "speaking score" for a student may be obtained by averaging all of the **Test 2** scores the student received in the class.

Achievement Tests
Unit 1

Name: _____

Date: _____

TEST 1

A. ☐1 *Listen to the excerpt. Mark each sentence **T** (true) or **F** (false).*

_____ 1. Gabrielle Spiegel thinks there are only two things you need to survive—honesty and a sense of humor.

_____ 2. Spiegel would rather spend her time reading novels than reading newspapers.

_____ 3. According to Spiegel, children and adults need time to watch television alone.

☐2 *Listen to the excerpt again. Then read the sentences. The underlined words are incorrect. Write the correct words.*

1. Gabrielle Spiegel teaches <u>English</u> at Johns Hopkins University.

   Correct word: _____

2. Spiegel's main area of interest and expertise is <u>modern</u> history.

   Correct word: _____

3. Spiegel <u>doesn't have</u> children.

   Correct word: _____

4. Spiegel used to have what she called <u>the Silent</u> hour with her children.

   Correct word: _____

B. *Listen to the sentences. Circle the meaning of the words you hear.*

1. a. anger   b. hopelessness   c. fear
2. a. ideas   b. dreams   c. preconceived notions
3. a. solution   b. prevention   c. partner
4. a. information   b. installation   c. consumption
5. a. deadly   b. unusual   c. illegal
6. a. excites   b. inspires   c. stops from doing anything productive

7. **a.** interesting   **b.** comforting   **c.** frightening
8. **a.** very boring   **b.** very painful   **c.** very interesting
9. **a.** leave the room   **b.** distrust   **c.** avoid becoming
   affected by
10. **a.** hobby   **b.** subject   **c.** goal

C. *Listen to the sentences. Write the auxiliary verb or contraction you hear.*

1. My friend, Myra, _____ become a news resister.

2. We _____ tried to convince her that her decision to stop reading and
   watching the news is a bit extreme.

3. It _____ been really difficult to make her listen to us.

4. I guess all those crime reports _____ really gotten to her.

5. Come to think of it, news stories _____ really too violent and
   depressing at times.

D. *Listen to the sentences. The passive voice is used. Write the verb tense you hear.*

| base form | present | present progressive | present perfect |
| past | past perfect | future | |

1. _____   5. _____
2. _____   6. _____
3. _____   7. _____
4. _____   8. _____

TEST 2

Topic: Talk about an interesting story that you've read, heard, or seen in the
news lately.

• Why did it catch your attention?

• What did you think and feel as you were reading it?

• What other information did you want to know that wasn't included in the
  report?

Achievement Tests
Unit 2

Name: _____

Date: _____

TEST 1

A. ☐1 *Listen to the excerpt. Mark each sentence **T** (true) or **F** (false).*

_____ 1. Helen Keller lost her sight and hearing in an accident.

_____ 2. As a child, Keller was angry and frustrated by her inability to understand others and express herself.

_____ 3. The speaker lost her eyesight when she was a baby.

_____ 4. Like Keller, she was angry and frustrated about her inability to understand and communicate with others.

☐2 *Listen to the excerpt again. Then read the sentences. The underlined words are incorrect. Write the correct words.*

1. Growing up, Helen Keller would touch the <u>hands</u> of others around her to find out what they were saying.

   Correct word: _____

2. At times, the young Keller would get so <u>happy</u> that she would kick and scream.

   Correct word: _____

3. Born prematurely, the speaker spent time in <u>a nursing home</u>.

   Correct word: _____

4. She flunked first grade because <u>spelling</u> didn't make sense to her.

   Correct word: _____

B. *Listen to the conversation. Circle the meaning of the words you hear.*

1. **a.** to succeed in controlling a problem
   b. to be defeated by a problem

2. **a.** something that improves your abilities
   b. something that keeps you from going beyond your abilities

3. **a.** facts that prove something is true
   b. the total amount of something

4. **a.** to know
   b. to ignore

5. **a.** intelligence to learn things
   b. determination to keep trying

6. **a.** sympathy
   b. intelligence

7. **a.** a surprise party
   b. a hidden fact that becomes known

8. **a.** to have the ability to do something
   b. to have the ability to move from one place to another

9. **a.** to fly very high or fast
   b. to run very quickly

10. **a.** an arrangement of plants and flowers
    b. a view across an area of land

 C. *Listen to the sentences and key expressions. Circle whether the expression has a **figurative** or a **literal** meaning.*

    1. **a.** figurative   **b.** literal
    2. **a.** figurative   **b.** literal
    3. **a.** figurative   **b.** literal
    4. **a.** figurative   **b.** literal

 D. *Listen to each sentence, and circle each thought group.*

1. It was Leila's first time using crutches and she had a difficult time turning around.

2. Sales of the new wheelchair have been so strong that the company is turning around and is number one in sales again.

3. It's difficult for my grandmother, who has arthritis, to reach deep down into the washing machine to remove clothes.

4. If you want to accomplish great deeds, you have to reach deep down into yourself and bring out the best in yourself.

E. *Listen to the excerpt. Complete each sentence with the gerund or infinitive form of one of the words below.*

walk   enter   install   know

1. We need _____ about the special needs of some members of our community.

2. Ramps at building entrances make it easier for people using wheelchairs _____ buildings.

3. If _____ up and down the stairs is difficult for you, a mechanical lift is useful.

4. We can alert the deaf or the hearing-impaired by _____ strobe lights on smoke and burglar alarms.

TEST 2

Topic: Describe someone you know of who has a disability and how he or she has overcome it.

- How do you know about this person's story?

- What is the significance of this person's story to your life?

- If you had the resources and the capability to help this person, what would you do?

Achievement Tests
Unit 3

Name: _____

Date: _____

TEST 1

 A. [1] *Listen to the interview. Circle the sentence that best expresses each main idea.*

1. **a.** Medical workers work too many hours a week.
   b. Medical workers sleep too many hours a week.

2. **a.** Worker fatigue due to lack of sleep results in serious problems in the health profession.
   b. Worker fatigue due to lack of sleep results in health professionals losing their jobs.

3. **a.** There are rules covering work hours but they are not strict.
   b. There are no rules covering work hours.

4. **a.** We need to give medical workers higher pay to get them to work longer.
   b. We need to raise public awareness to make getting enough sleep a priority.

 [2] *Listen to the interview again. Mark each sentence **T** (true) or **F** (false).*

_____ 1. Medical residents and interns can work up to 100 hours a week.

_____ 2. When medical workers work up to 100 hours a week, they perform their jobs effectively.

_____ 3. An intern is allowed to work for 16 hours a day for 6 days.

_____ 4. Surgeons and anesthesiologists can be on call for many nights every week.

B. *Listen to the conversation. Circle the word or phrase that best completes each sentence.*

1. **a.** scared   **b.** glad   **c.** irritable
2. **a.** sleep-induced   **b.** sleep-deprived **c.** sleep-in
3. **a.** accumulates   **b.** accelerates   **c.** accentuates
4. **a.** shy   **b.** miserable   **c.** monstrous
5. **a.** drooping   **b.** twisting   **c.** turning
6. **a.** smoking   **b.** singing   **c.** snoring
7. **a.** aggressive   **b.** alert   **c.** amused
8. **a.** out of sync   **b.** out of sight   **c.** out of tune
9. **a.** suspend   **b.** suspect   **c.** sustain
10. **a.** do alone   **b.** do again   **c.** do without

C. *Listen to the sentences. Circle the contrasted words.*

1. Your eyes are looking at me, but your mind is somewhere else.

2. My children sleep a little, but wake up a lot.

3. Joshua takes naps all the time, but his wife never does.

4. These are common effects of sleep deprivation, but they have serious consequences.

5. Teenagers have surges of energy at night and waves of sleepiness during the day.

 D. *Listen to the **if**-clauses. Use the words given, and write the result clause.*

1. feel / you / sleepy / would / less

   _____

2. might / for / children / she / more / have / her / time

   _____

3. during / alert / operations / be / more / would / they

   _____

4. in / teenagers / attentive / might / more / be / school

   _____

5. at / I / night / better / sleep / could

   _____

6. before / could / manager / work / to / his / get / he

   _____

7. been / have / promoted / would / she

   _____

TEST 2

Topic: Describe a situation in which you had to stay awake for a long period of time.

- What did you do to keep yourself awake?

- Describe the sensations and emotions that you felt as you went without sleep for a long time.

- When did you finally get to sleep? Did you fall asleep immediately or not? What did you do to make yourself sleep?

- How did you feel after you woke up?

Achievement Tests
Unit 4

Name: _____

Date: _____

TEST 1

A. **1** *Listen to the excerpt. Mark each sentence **T** (true) or **F** (false).*

_____ 1. In the morning of the hurricane, the sky was dark and it was raining very hard.

_____ 2. By mid-afternoon, the winds turned violent and a wall of water rolled in from the sea to the shore.

_____ 3. People were repeatedly warned of the hurricane by weather forecasters but chose to stay in the area.

_____ 4. The hurricane caused a flood that destroyed lives and property.

2 *Listen to the excerpt again. Then read the sentences. The underlined words are incorrect. Write the correct words.*

1. People called their friends to come and watch the <u>sunset</u>.

Correct word: _____

2. People sat outside on their <u>lawns</u>.

Correct word: _____

3. People watched in <u>delight</u> as a wall of water rolled in.

Correct word: _____

4. Some of the houses <u>fell down</u> when the water hit.

Correct word: _____

B. *Listen to the sentences. Circle the meaning of the words you hear.*

1. **a.** nervous   **b.** sleepy   **c.** quiet

2. **a.** surge   **b.** supply   **c.** failure

3. **a.** easily seen   **b.** easily hurt   **c.** easily heard

4. **a.** instructions   **b.** directions   **c.** supplies

5. **a.** to feel a sudden hunger   **b.** to feel a sudden sadness   **c.** to feel a sudden fear or anxiety

6. **a.** technologically advanced   **b.** medically tested   **c.** artistically done

7. **a.** moving to a safer place   **b.** moving to a smaller place   **c.** moving to a dangerous place

8. **a.** to label extra supplies   **b.** to buy or save extra supplies   **c.** to list extra supplies

9. **a.** presentation   **b.** preview   **c.** prediction

10. **a.** very difficult   **b.** very dangerous   **c.** very important

 C. *Listen to the sentences. Circle the adjective form that correctly completes each sentence.*

1. **a.** amazed
   b. amazing

2. **a.** heartened
   b. heartening

3. **a.** frightened
   b. frightening

4. **a.** surprised
   b. surprising

D. *Listen to the sentences. Underline the items that are listed. Draw arrows to show rising and falling intonation.*

1. In his lifetime, Miguel has experienced hurricanes, floods, landslides, forest fires, and droughts.

2. The different parts of a hurricane are: the eye of the storm, the eye wall, and the hurricane's tail.

3. By the time the forest fire was put out, 181 people were dead, 253 were injured, 8,500 were left homeless, and $150 million worth of property was destroyed.

4. We have no electricity, no water, no food, and no warm clothes.

E. *Listen to the sentences. Circle the adjective clause that correctly completes each sentence.*

1. **a.** who worked 14-hour shifts
   b. which lasted for two days

2. **a.** when the drought was in its fifth month
   b. who helped them a great deal

3. **a.** which was planted late
   b. where many cornfields are located

4. **a.** whose predictions are usually accurate
   b. when he learned it would stop raining

TEST 2

Topic: What could you do to help a friend who has just been through a major disaster?

• What material things would you be willing to offer?

• What tasks, errands, or services would you be willing to do?

• Would you offer the same assistance to a complete stranger? Why or why not?

Achievement Tests
Unit 5

Name: _____

Date: _____

TEST 1

A.   1   *Listen to the excerpt. Circle the sentence that best expresses the main idea.*

1. a. Residents in Truro have had to think of new ways to dispose of their trash.
   b. Residents in Truro have had to start paying to dispose of their trash.

2. a. Residents are now burning and burying trash in landfills in eastern Massachusetts.
   b. Residents are recycling and reusing what was once thought of as trash.

3. a. Recycling is popular among the town's residents.
   b. Recycling is expensive.

2   *Listen to the excerpt again. Circle the correct answer.*

1. What is yard waste now made into?
   a. grass
   b. compost

2. What is now done with recyclable plastics?
   a. They are sold to a recycling company.
   b. They are taken to a separate landfill.

3. What does the "swap shop" allow people to do?
   a. It allows people to sell unwanted items.
   b. People can leave things so that others can take them.

4. What is a common activity at the "dump dance"?
   a. a picnic
   b. a sound and light show

B. *Listen to each sentence. Circle the meaning of the words you hear.*

1. a. compete with
   b. kill
   c. worship

2. a. collect
   b. wind up
   c. blow around

3. a. sometimes
   b. expensive
   c. total

4. **a.** natural
   b. holy
   c. expensive

5. **a.** cheaply
   b. quickly
   c. by hand

 C. *Listen to the excerpts. Circle the word that best completes each sentence.*

1. **a.** competitor
   b. competitive
   c. competitively

2. **a.** wasted
   b. wasteful
   c. wastefully

3. **a.** industrial
   b. industrialize
   c. industrialized

4. **a.** protection
   b. protect
   c. protected

5. **a.** recycling
   b. recycle
   c. recycled

 D. *Listen to the words. Circle the word you hear.*

1. **a.** sink	**b.** think	**c.** zinc
2. **a.** sought	**b.** taught	**c.** thought
3. **a.** dread	**b.** thread	**c.** tread
4. **a.** sews	**b.** those	**c.** toes
5. **a.** pass	**b.** pat	**c.** path

E. *Listen to each dialogue. Circle the sentence that best sums up each conversation.*

1. **a.** Rom could have taken them back for money.
   b. Rom shouldn't have gotten a refund.

2. **a.** Mick ought to have waited another month to change oil.
   b. Mick shouldn't have let the oil spill on the ground.

3. **a.** Kizza could have recycled the milk cartons.
   b. Kizza shouldn't have bought milk in non-recyclable containers.

4. **a.** Toti couldn't have burned the leaves.
   b. Toti should have raked the leaves.

5. **a.** Alan shouldn't have thrown out the old lumber.
   b. Alan couldn't have used the old lumber to build shelves.

F. *Listen to each dialogue. Circle the word or phrase that best completes each sentence.*

1. Eric _____ glass from his burnable garbage.
   a. should have separated
   b. separated
   c. will not separate

2. Rex _____ his old newspapers to the local school.
   a. gave
   b. would give
   c. couldn't have given

3. Nicole _____ a brand new hybrid car.
   a. bought
   b. will buy
   c. should have bought

TEST 2

Topic: Describe a memorable experience that you've had with nature.

- Was it a pleasant or an unpleasant experience?

- Did you learn something new as a result of this experience? What was it?

- If it were to happen again, what would you do differently?

Achievement Tests
Unit 6

Name: _____

Date: _____

TEST 1

A. **1** *Listen to the excerpt. Mark each sentence **T** (true) or **F** (false).*

_____ 1. Only a few Americans donate to charity and do volunteer work.

_____ 2. There are four types of philanthropists.

_____ 3. People and institutions give away their time and money to help others and to help themselves.

_____ 4. Whether it is because of concern for others or concern for themselves, philanthropists desire change in the world.

2 *Listen to the excerpt again. Circle the word or phrase that best completes each sentence.*

1. In the United States today, not-for-profit organizations and charities number about _____.
   a. 1 million   b. 2 million   c. 3 million

2. Foundations are organized by individuals who are _____.
   a. very busy   b. very bored   c. very rich

3. Private corporations make donations or give away their _____ for free.
   a. profits   b. products and services   c. promotions

4. Aside from tax benefits, donors often receive _____ publicity.
   a. favorable   b. negative   c. very little

B. *Listen to the sentences and key words. Circle the meaning of the words you hear.*

1. a. an organization that helps people
   b. an organization that sings in church

2. a. join
   b. give

3. a. people who don't like to be with others
   b. people who show concern for others

4. a. money to pay a teacher's salary
   b. money to pay for a student's education

5. a. a person who receives a donation
   b. a person who donates something

6. a. shocked
   b. angered

7. **a.** a person who pays another to work for him
   b. a person who helps someone by giving money

8. **a.** money saved for later use
   b. money given to poor people

9. **a.** to prepare
   b. to promise to give

10. **a.** to borrow money
    b. to pay for

C. *Listen to the tag questions, and draw intonation lines. Mark each sentence **C** (comment) or* **Q** *(question) according to the intonation.*

_____ 1. Gladys Holm's $18 million donation will be used to fund heart disease research, won't it?

_____ 2. Bill Gates really cares about the world's poor children, doesn't he?

_____ 3. You must be at least 21 years old to be a fire brigade volunteer, mustn't you?

_____ 4. If your father were alive today, he'd be proud to see you helping people build houses, wouldn't he?

_____ 5. Philanthropists shouldn't always expect to be thanked for their efforts, should they?

_____ 6. Dress for Success doesn't only provide free clothing, does it?

D. *Complete each sentence with a tag question.*

1. _____?

2. _____?

3. _____?

4. _____?

5. _____?

6. _____?

TEST 2

Topic: Imagine you had a million dollars to give to charity. Which charitable organization would you give it to?

- Why did you choose this particular charity?

- How would you turn over your donation? In cash, check, or products worth a million dollars? Why?

- Would you want to have it publicized or would you do it anonymously? Why?

Achievement Tests
Unit 7

TEST 1

🎧 **A.** 1 *Listen to the excerpt. Mark each sentence **T** (true) or **F** (false).*

_____ 1. IQ tests have been commonly used in American schools.

_____ 2. IQ tests give a fairly accurate prediction of a person's success in life.

_____ 3. A person's emotional intelligence is more important than his or her IQ, according to American psychologist Daniel Goleman.

🎧 2 *Listen to the excerpt again. Circle the correct sentence in each pair.*

1. **a.** IQ tests have been criticized for one basic reason.
   b. IQ tests have been criticized for several reasons.

2. **a.** IQ tests accurately predict a person's success in life.
   b. IQ tests do not accurately predict a person's success in life.

3. **a.** The number of unemployed men who had an above-average IQ was the same as the number of unemployed men who scored below average.
   b. The number of unemployed men who had an above-average IQ was higher than the number of unemployed men who scored below average.

4. **a.** EQ includes skills such as relating to other people.
   b. EQ includes skills such as predicting other people's intelligence.

🎧 **B.** *Listen to each dialogue. Circle the sentence that best sums up each conversation.*

1. **a.** Barb thinks Nat shouldn't complain.
   b. Barb thinks Nat should be perceptive.

2. **a.** Jane should act with respect toward her grandfather.
   b. Jane should try to understand her grandfather.

3. **a.** Ken thinks Eric has to accept disappointments.
   b. Ken thinks Eric should be angry.

4. **a.** Jan will not be hurt and angry about Kay's promotion.
   b. Jan will not talk to Kay.

5. **a.** Mary Ann is a happy and excited person.
   b. Mary Ann thinks she is important.

6. **a.** Gwen wanted to discuss the advice.
   b. Gwen had a negative reaction to the advice.

7. **a.** Don is easygoing.
   b. Don makes allowances for other people.

8. **a.** It's difficult for Francis to admit he was wrong.
   b. Francis studied, but he forgot everything he learned.

 C. *Listen to the words. Put a dot over the syllable with the strongest stress. Write a schwa [ə] over the vowels that are pronounced "uh."*

1. in•tel•li•gence

2. en•thu•si•asm

3. ne•ga•tive

4. un•em•ployed

5. em•pa•thy

6. al•low•an•ces

7. po•si•tive

 D. *Listen to each statement. Circle the sentence that expresses the statement in indirect speech.*

1. **a.** He told me that his IQ is 140.
   b. He told me that his IQ was 140.

2. **a.** She said she might need to stay late at work this evening.
   b. She said she would need to stay late at work this evening.

3. **a.** She told me that Marty has gone to the hockey game on Saturday.
   b. She told me that Marty was going to the hockey game on Saturday.

4. **a.** I was told that I might take the IQ test.
   b. I was told that I had to take the IQ test.

5. **a.** He said that Nicki was studying psychology in college.
   b. He said that Nicki had studied psychology in college.

6. **a.** He said that he had to take the IQ test tomorrow.
   b. He said that he should take the IQ test tomorrow.

7. **a.** She asked me if I ever took an EQ test.
   b. She asked me if I had ever taken an EQ test.

8. **a.** He said that Mensa welcomed people whose IQ is in the top 2 percent.
   b. He said that Mensa would welcome people whose IQ is in the top 2 percent.

TEST 2

Topic: In which of the five skills of emotional intelligence—self-awareness, self-control, self-motivation, empathy, people skills—do you think you need the most improvement?

• Why do you think you need to improve in this area?

• Describe an instance when you realized your weakness in this area.

• What are some of the things you could do to improve this skill?

Achievement Tests
Unit 8

Name: _____

Date: _____

TEST 1

A. 1 *Listen to the telephone conversations. Complete each sentence with the correct name.*

1. _____ invited Julie to have lunch with him at the new sandwich place.

2. Julie called off her lunch date with _____.

3. Bill only wants to date _____.

2 *Listen to the conversations again. Mark each sentence **T** (true) or **F** (false).*

_____ 1. Stephen wants to do homework with Julie.

_____ 2. Stephen was thinking of eating a baguette sandwich with Julie at Au Pain Gourmet.

_____ 3. Bill was planning to cook lunch for Julie.

_____ 4. Julie told Bill she was working on a science project that she had to submit by Monday.

B. *Listen to the sentences and key words. Circle the meaning of the words you hear.*

1. **a.** bread   **b.** money   **c.** flour

2. **a.** problems developing   **b.** friendship developing   **c.** plans developing

3. **a.** created   **b.** ended   **c.** moved

4. **a.** something to eat   **b.** something to think about   **c.** something to sell

5. **a.** baker   **b.** housekeeper   **c.** salary earner

6. **a.** It's better to get more help.   **b.** It's better to do less things.   **c.** It's better to do things alone.

7. **a.** to decorate a house   **b.** to make money   **c.** to take a vacation

8. **a.** to be very creative   **b.** to be very happy   **c.** to be very serious

9. **a.** main source of income   **b.** favorite cooking activity   **c.** staple food

10. **a.** selling   **b.** buying   **c.** changing

C. *Listen to the words. Pay attention to the sound of the underlined letters.*

> s<u>o</u>me /ə/
> g<u>oo</u>d /ʊ/
> c<u>o</u>ld /ow/
> h<u>o</u>t /ɑ/
> f<u>oo</u>d /uw/

Now listen to these words. Circle the letter of the symbol with the same sound as the underlined letters.

1. oni<u>o</u>n
   a. /ɑ/
   b. /ə/

2. c<u>oo</u>kie
   a. /uw/
   b. /ʊ/

3. y<u>o</u>gurt
   a. /ow/
   b. /ə/

4. p<u>o</u>t
   a. /ɑ/
   b. /ow/

5. n<u>oo</u>dles
   a. /ʊ/
   b. /uw/

 D. *Listen to the conversations. Write the phrasal verb from the list below that best completes each conversation.*

| turn (it) down | call back | run into | put (it) off |
| turn (it) on | call (it) off | ask (him) over | try (it) out |

1. _____

2. _____

3. _____

4. _____

5. _____

6. _____

7. _____

8. _____

TEST 2

Topic: Describe a strange, exotic, or unique dish that you have eaten.

- What was the situation? Where and when did it happen? Who were you with?

- What were the ingredients of the dish, and how was it prepared and served?

- What did it taste like? How did you feel after eating it?

Achievement Tests
Unit 9

Name: _____

Date: _____

TEST 1

A. ☐1 *Listen to the excerpt. Mark each sentence **T** (true) or **F** (false).*

_____ 1. Esteban's family moved from Mexico to the United States.

_____ 2. Esteban quickly adjusted to life in the United States.

_____ 3. Esteban felt frustrated that he couldn't speak English well.

_____ 4. Esteban was unhappy in school and at home.

☐2 *Listen to the excerpt again. Circle the correct answer.*

1. What was Esteban like when his family lived in Mexico?
   a. Shy and studious.
   b. Active and outgoing.
   c. Aggressive and resentful.

2. How old was Esteban when his family moved?
   a. 12
   b. 14
   c. 16

3. What did Esteban's teachers suggest to help him?
   a. They suggested that he join clubs to meet other students.
   b. They suggested that he take extra English classes after school.
   c. They suggested that he talk to the school psychologist.

4. How did Esteban deal with his unhappiness at home?
   a. He talked about it with his family.
   b. He pretended to be sick.
   c. He suppressed his sad feelings.

B. *Listen to the statements and read the corresponding sentences below. Circle whether the meaning is the same or different from the statements you hear.*

1. German is Emma's first language.	same	different
2. Frank's family is very close.	same	different
3. Jon will study Japanese this weekend.	same	different
4. Yoshino was happy to get her visa.	same	different
5. Speaking a new language to a native speaker is fun.	same	different
6. Ken's language skills set him apart from his classmates.	same	different
7. Immigrant communities will continue to grow and develop in America.	same	different
8. Many immigrants have been uprooted from their home countries.	same	different

 C. *Listen to the words. Pay attention to the sound of the underlined letters.*

immigration	/ʃ/
decision	/ʒ/
culture	/tʃ/
language	/dʒ/

Now listen to these words. Circle the symbol with the same sound as the underlined letters.

1. natural
   a. /tʃ/
   b. /ʃ/

2. extension
   a. /ʃ/
   b. /tʃ/

3. refugee
   a. /dʒ/
   b. /ʒ/

4. Asia
   a. /dʒ/
   b. /ʒ/

5. deportation
   a. /ʃ/
   b. /dʒ/

6. Caucasian
   a. /ʃ/
   b. /ʒ/

 D. *Listen to the sentences. Circle **same** if the statement uses only one verb tense. Circle **contrasting** if the statement uses more than one verb tense.*

1. **a.** same   **b.** contrasting
2. **a.** same   **b.** contrasting
3. **a.** same   **b.** contrasting
4. **a.** same   **b.** contrasting
5. **a.** same   **b.** contrasting
6. **a.** same   **b.** contrasting
7. **a.** same   **b.** contrasting
8. **a.** same   **b.** contrasting

TEST 2

Topic: Agree or disagree with the following.

"If the parents of a child speak different languages, the child should be brought up learning his mother's language first."

• Cite the reasons for your position.

• What other factors influence or determine the language that a child learns?

• What do you think is the ideal age for a child to start learning a second language? Why?

Achievement Tests
Unit 10

Name: _____

Date: _____

TEST 1

 A. ☐1 *Listen to the excerpt. Circle the sentence that best expresses each main idea.*

    1. a. The sound of sirens at night prompted many New Yorkers to call for a ban on sirens.

    b. The sound of car alarms at night prompted many New Yorkers to call for a ban on car alarms.

    2. a. A group of New Yorkers has come up with measures to call attention to or punish owners of cars whose alarms go off at night.

    b. Most New Yorkers have come up with measures to call attention to or punish owners of cars whose alarms go off at night.

    3. a. Noise negatively affects the health and quality of life of adults.

    b. Noise negatively affects the health and quality of life of children and adults.

    4. a. Enforcement of existing and new laws may be increasing noise in some neighborhoods.

    b. Enforcement of existing and new laws may be cutting down noise in some neighborhoods.

☐2 *Listen to the excerpt again. Circle the fact that is **not** in the excerpt.*

    1. Some nasty city sounds are _____.

    a. sirens
    b. jackhammers
    c. thunder

    2. Some retaliatory measures against owners of cars whose alarms go off are _____.

    a. removing the alarms
    b. breaking an egg on the windshield or front hood
    c. smearing Vaseline all over the windshield

    3. Noise affects people's _____.

    a. ability to sleep
    b. ability to breathe
    c. ability to work

B. *Listen to each sentence. Circle the meaning of the word or phrase you hear.*

1. **a.** to destroy
   b. to stop
   c. to remind

2. **a.** to throw someone into the water
   b. to jump over someone
   c. to make someone very angry

3. **a.** to fall down
   b. to start making noise
   c. to smell bad

4. **a.** echoes
   b. movements
   c. sounds

5. **a.** to cause
   b. to stop
   c. to repeat

6. **a.** to laugh
   b. to return
   c. to startle

7. **a.** to sell
   b. to remove
   c. to fix

8. **a.** constant
   b. strange
   c. slight

9. **a.** to allow
   b. to prohibit
   c. to punish

10. **a.** an unofficial group of people who catch criminals
    b. retired policemen
    c. a group of young women

C. *Listen to the excerpt. Circle the particles that are stressed.*

> I think they're bullies. They walk around in a group and show off by destroying other people's property. They think they can just act up and no one will fight back. Well, I'm fed up. I'm taking them to court.

 D. *Listen to the sentences. Circle the verb tense used in each sentence.*

1. **a.** simple future   **b.** future perfect   **c.** future progressive
2. **a.** simple future   **b.** future perfect   **c.** future progressive
3. **a.** simple future   **b.** future perfect   **c.** future progressive
4. **a.** simple future   **b.** future perfect   **c.** future progressive
5. **a.** simple future   **b.** future perfect   **c.** future progressive
6. **a.** simple future   **b.** future perfect   **c.** future progressive
7. **a.** simple future   **b.** future perfect   **c.** future progressive
8. **a.** simple future   **b.** future perfect   **c.** future progressive

---

TEST 2

Topic: Describe what your perfect day would be if you had the latest technology.

- Where would you be spending the day?
- Would you be spending it alone or with others? Why?
- What would be the high point of your day?

Achievement Tests
Test 1 Audioscript

UNIT 1

A

1 *Listen to the excerpt. Mark each sentence **T** (true) or **F** (false).*

Margot Adler: Academia turns out to be a place filled with news resisters. Take Gabrielle Spiegel, the chair of the history department at Johns Hopkins University. Perhaps it's understandable that a medievalist who says her period of study ends around 1328 would find daily news, in her words, "ephemeral, repetitive and inconsequential."

Gabrielle Spiegel: But I think my underlying reason is that, you know, life is short. There's only a certain amount of time that you have to spend on things, and I have always believed that there are two things you really need to get through life, and I say this to my children in a sort of nauseatingly repetitive way. The first is a really rich fantasy life so you can imagine what the possibilities are, and the other is a sense of humor so you can deal with what is. And actually I'd rather spend my time on my fantasy life and reading novels than reading newspapers. And I really do think that's why I don't read newspapers.

I think we live in a society that offers us very, very little time alone. And the way children are raised, you know, set in front of televisions, they don't have a lot of time to be by themselves. When my children were little, we used to have a thing called Mommy's hour in which, you know, they had to go in their rooms and just think for an hour or two a day so I could think for an hour or two a day.

2 *Listen to the excerpt again. Then read the sentences. The underlined words are incorrect. Write the correct words.*

B

Listen to the sentences. Circle the meaning of the words you hear.

1. According to Tupton Shudrun, the media make us feel like things are bad and can't get any better. This despair keeps us from actually doing something for ourselves and for others.
2. Some reporters show biases in their writing that may influence their readers.
3. Reading books instead of newspapers is the perfect remedy for boredom.
4. I've been watching bad news on TV all week and I've had enough. I think my news intake has exceeded my capacity to understand it.
5. Instead of exposing the personal lives of celebrities, the media can better serve the public by reporting on lethal drugs that have taken people's lives.

6. Too much television reduces us to sitting and watching things happen. It immobilizes us.
7. A number of people find it soothing to watch corn grow. Other people think it's relaxing to watch pretty fish swim around a tank.
8. Given a choice, some people would rather watch corn grow than watch the news the whole day. Frankly, I don't see what's so riveting about a field of corn.
9. These days, watching the evening news isn't at all pleasant. I think I'll stop watching the news all together and just disengage.
10. When Arnold was a young boy, his pastime was collecting autographs of people he saw in the news. Now, he owns a shop that buys and sells autographs of famous people.

C

Listen to the sentences. Write the auxiliary verb or contraction you hear.

1. My friend, Myra, has become a news resister.
2. We've tried to convince her that her decision to stop reading and watching the news is a bit extreme.
3. It's been really difficult to make her listen to us.
4. I guess all those crime reports have really gotten to her.
5. Come to think of it, news stories're really too violent and depressing at times.

D

Listen to the sentences. The passive voice is used. Write the verb tense you hear.

1. Hi. I'm Douglas O'Brian, reporting today from Iowa, where millions of people are being sheltered in temporary accommodations following a severe storm that has left thousands stranded.
2. Emergency service was provided late into the night as water levels rose.
3. Many people have been treated for shock.
4. Meanwhile, everyone is urged to stay calm and remain alert.
5. In other news, Francisco Olloa was rescued by his dog, Ted, last Friday after he fell through the ice into the pond.
6. People had been warned by news reports that the ice was thin, but Francisco did not hear the reports.
7. Francisco said that Ted should be given a medal for his heroic rescue.
8. We just learned from our sources at City Hall that Ted will be awarded a brand new collar with a miniature medal by the mayor himself.

UNIT 2

A

1 *Listen to the excerpt. Mark each sentence **T** (true) or **F** (false).*

Helen Keller was less than two years old when she came down with a fever. It struck dramatically and left her unconscious. The fever went just as suddenly. But she was blinded and, very soon after, deaf. As she grew up, she managed to learn to do tiny errands, but she also realized that she was missing something. "Sometimes," she later wrote, "I stood between two persons who were conversing and touched their lips. I could not understand, and was vexed. I moved my lips and gesticulated frantically without result. This made me so angry at times that I kicked and screamed until I was exhausted." She was a wild child.

I can understand her rage. I was born two months prematurely and was placed in an incubator. The practice at the time was to pump a large amount of oxygen into the incubator, something doctors have since learned to be extremely cautious about. But as a result, I lost my sight. I was sent to a state school for the blind, but I flunked first grade because Braille just didn't make any sense to me. Words were a weird concept. I remember being hit and slapped. And you act all that in. All rage is anger that is acted in, bottled in for so long that it just pops out.

2 *Listen to the excerpt again. Then read the sentences. The underlined words are incorrect. Write the correct words.*

B

Listen to the conversation. Circle the meaning of the words you hear.

1. **Mark:** You know, every time I hear Diane Shuur, I'm amazed at how she has managed to <u>overcome</u> her handicap.
2. **Ruby:** She hates the word "handicap." She says her blindness was never a <u>limitation</u> to what she could achieve.
3. **Mark:** She's right. The fact that she's won two Grammy awards, recorded more than a dozen albums, performed around the world, and was awarded the Helen Keller Achievement Award is <u>proof</u> that she's truly a winner many times over.
4. **Ruby:** Helen Keller didn't like to be called handicapped either. She believed she was just like everybody else and wanted people to <u>recognize</u> that.
5. **Mark:** Well, I think her <u>perseverance</u> in mastering language went beyond the ordinary.
6. **Ruby:** She was lucky to have been tutored by Annie Sullivan. Annie was patient and had a lot of <u>compassion</u>. She understood Helen's anger and frustration.
7. **Mark:** It must have been a moment of <u>revelation</u> to Helen Keller when she first realized words were related to things.
8. **Ruby:** Maybe that's what Diane Shuur felt, too, when she finally understood Braille. But, I guess it

was music that really <u>empowered</u> her to break out of her rage and isolation.
9. **Mark:** Yeah! Maybe that's why her songs often give me a feeling of lightness and freedom, of wanting to <u>soar</u> above the ground and reach for the sky.
10. **Ruby:** Me, too! Her songs make me imagine myself flying over a beautiful <u>landscape</u> of trees and mountains.

C

Listen to the sentences and key expressions. Circle whether the expression has a figurative or a literal meaning.

1. Mechanical lifts make it easier for people to <u>get to the top</u> of buildings.
2. Many of Emily's colleagues believed she wouldn't <u>get to the top</u> of the company because she was a woman.
3. Even those who thought Crista wouldn't <u>make it</u> through high school stood up and cheered for her as she wheeled herself up to the stage to receive her diploma.
4. Saeid's mother was afraid he would hurt himself while building the cabinet, but she let him <u>make it</u> without any help from her.

D

Listen to each sentence, and circle each thought group.

1. It was Leila's first time using crutches and she had a difficult time turning around.
2. Sales of the new wheelchair have been so strong that the company is turning around and is number one in sales again.
3. It's difficult for my grandmother, who has arthritis, to reach deep down into the washing machine to remove clothes.
4. If you want to accomplish great deeds, you have to reach deep down into yourself and bring out the best in yourself.

E

Listen to the excerpt. Complete each sentence with the gerund or infinitive form of one of the words below.

It's important to know about the special needs of some members of our community in order to make life safer and more comfortable for them. For example, entrance ramps to buildings make it easier for people using wheelchairs to enter buildings. For those who find walking up and down the stairs difficult, mechanical lifts are very useful. Installing strobe lights on smoke and burglar alarms will ensure that those who are deaf or hearing-impaired will be alerted to dangerous situations.

UNIT 3

A _____

1 *Listen to the interview. Circle the sentence that best expresses each main idea.*

Sleep Researcher: Thank you for taking time to share your experience with me. Can you tell me about the sleep problems that medical workers have?

Medical Worker: Well, one of the problems is that medical residents and interns can work up to 100 hours a week. They can get really overtired. If they worked less, they wouldn't get so tired.

SR: And does this fatigue cause serious problems in the health profession?

MW: Sure. Just think about your own work. How well would you do your job if you slept only five or six hours a night?

SR: Aren't there any rules about how much you can work?

MW: Yes, but they are not strict enough. For example, if interns showed up for work 6 days, and worked for 16 hours, they would be following regulations, as long as they worked less the following week.

SR: That's terrible! What can be done to make getting sleep a priority?

MW: We need to raise public awareness. For example, surgeons and anesthesiologists can be on call for many nights every week. If they weren't allowed to do that, there would be fewer problems.

2 *Listen to the interview again. Mark each sentence **T** (true) or **F** (false).*

B _____

Listen to the conversation. Circle the word or phrase that best completes each sentence.

1. **Taron:** What's the matter, Rob? You don't seem too happy these days, especially in the morning, when you're quite _____.
2. **Rob:** Oh, I don't know, Taron. I guess it's because I haven't gotten much sleep lately. I'm what you might call _____.
3. **Taron:** That's too bad. You know, I read somewhere that when people lack sleep night after night, they develop a sleep debt. The number of hours that they lack sleep _____.
4. **Rob:** Really? You mean, I owe my body hours of sleep? No wonder I haven't been feeling right lately. Sometimes it's so bad, I feel completely _____.
5. **Taron:** I can tell from the way you look and the way you can't seem to stand or sit up straight. Your head and your body always seem to be _____.
6. **Rob:** Not only that, but the minute I get the chance to sit somewhere, my eyes start blinking, I start yawning, and pretty soon, I'm fast asleep and _____.
7. **Taron:** I hate to tell you this, but others have started noticing that, too. You fall asleep even during meetings and presentations when you should be fully _____.
8. **Rob:** I know, I know. But I can't help it. I'm wide awake until the early morning hours and then feel sleepy throughout the day. My whole system is _____.
9. **Taron:** You're probably one of those people who suffer from insomnia. At least, that's what I _____.
10. **Rob:** You could be right. I think it's about time I see a doctor. I can't take any more of this. Sleep is something I can't _____.

C _____

Listen to the sentences. Circle the contrasted words.

1. Your eyes are looking at me, but your mind is somewhere else.
2. My children sleep a little, but wake up a lot.
3. Joshua takes naps all the time, but his wife never does.
4. These are common effects of sleep deprivation, but they have serious consequences.
5. Teenagers have surges of energy at night and waves of sleepiness during the day.

D _____

*Listen to the **if**-clauses. Use the words given and write the result clause.*

1. If you took regular naps, . . .
2. If Marilyn didn't work the night shift, . . .
3. If surgeons weren't on call for many nights a week, . . .
4. If classes started at 9:00 A.M., . . .
5. If I didn't drink so much cola and coffee, . . .
6. If Ernesto didn't sleep so late, . . .
7. If Joan weren't such a daydreamer, . . .

UNIT 4

A _____

1 *Listen to the excerpt. Mark each sentence **T** (true) or **F** (false).*

The morning of the hurricane, the weather was deceptively pleasant, though a bit windy, on Long Island, New York. Some beachside residents telephoned their friends who lived inland and invited them to come and watch the huge waves that were beginning to roll in from the Atlantic. People sat outside on their porches and enjoyed the view. However, by mid-afternoon the sky had grown dark, and violent winds began to blow with such intensity that garden furniture sailed through the air, and pieces of houses began to break off and fly away. People watched in shock as a thick wall of clouds came in from the sea toward the shore. As it came closer, they realized they weren't looking at clouds at all; it was a wall of water!

Because there was little or no warning of the hurricane, people expected only some foul weather and didn't panic. They remained calm and stayed in the area until disaster struck. Then they were caught off guard. When the hurricane hit the shore, some houses were suddenly under 30 feet of water. According to surviving witnesses, some of the houses blew up when the water hit, as if from a bomb; others flew up into the air and crashed back into the water. Office workers later reported looking outside at the street, which was suddenly flooded. They saw desks, cars, and children's toys floating down the street, and they watched helplessly as people floated by, too.

[2] Listen to the excerpt again. Then read the sentences. The underlined words are incorrect. Write the correct words.

B _____

Listen to the sentences. Circle the meaning of the words you hear.

1. Nevelee has noticed that her dog, Sam, becomes jittery during bad storms.
2. Roberto grew up in a small town without electricity, so now, whenever there's a power outage, he thinks about his childhood.
3. People who live on a mountainside are vulnerable to storms, earthquakes, and landslides.
4. A good camper always carries provisions for emergency situations.
5. When you're inside a building during an earthquake, don't panic. Stay calm and consider your options.
6. Oftentimes, even the most sophisticated equipment is of little use in predicting the exact path of a cyclone.
7. "The moment the water reaches that mark," the mayor pointed to the line on the wall, "we should announce that everyone should start evacuating."
8. Since it was Armida's first time to stock up on winter supplies, she asked her sister-in-law to make her a list.
9. Leo's grandfather can give an accurate weather forecast just by looking at the sky and smelling the air around him.
10. Sheila was in charge of a vital task at the disaster relief department—gathering and distributing food supplies.

C _____

Listen to the sentences. Circle the adjective form that correctly completes each sentence.

1. The number of volunteers who came from all over the country to help rebuild the country was _____.
2. Even though the drought had reached its fifth month, people stayed hopeful and helped each other survive the crisis. Luca found this _____.
3. When Andrew explained that hail was only ice falling from the sky, Majid was no longer _____.
4. After last night's forecast of warm temperatures and sunny skies, today's snowfall is _____.

D _____

Listen to the sentences. Underline the items that are listed. Draw arrows to show rising and falling intonation.

1. In his lifetime, Miguel has experienced hurricanes, floods, landslides, forest fires, and droughts.
2. The different parts of a hurricane are: the eye of the storm, the eye wall, and the hurricane's tail.
3. By the time the forest fire was put out, 181 people were dead, 253 were injured, 8,500 were left homeless, and $150 million worth of property was destroyed.
4. We have no electricity, no water, no food, and no warm clothes.

E _____

Listen to the sentences. Circle the adjective clause that correctly completes each sentence.

1. The volunteers worked through the storm . . .
2. The people finally received donations from other countries in November . . .
3. The hailstorm ruined this year's harvest in Nebraska . . .
4. The farmers learned it would rain from the weather forecaster . . .

UNIT 5

A _____

[1] Listen to the excerpt. Circle the sentence that best expresses the main idea.

In the small town of Truro in eastern Massachusetts, space in the local landfill has run out; therefore, residents have had to think of new ways to dispose of their trash. With no room for items such as newspapers, bottles, and old lumber at the landfill, local residents have come up with many innovative programs to recycle and/or reuse what was once thought of as only trash. For instance, yard waste such as leaves and grass, which used to be thrown in the landfill, is now broken down and made into compost used by local people as fertilizer in their gardens. In addition, recyclable plastics, newspapers, bottles, and cans are sold to a recycling company, thereby bringing in revenue for the town. The most popular local innovation, though, has been the founding of a "swap shop." This is a building to which people bring their unwanted clothing, books, and toys so that others who need them can take them.

Since there is so much participation in all the recycling programs, the dump is seen as a place to meet with friends and neighbors and catch up on local news. There is even an annual September evening "dump dance," where locals dance to live music and have picnics by candlelight at the dump. This has become a highlight of the summer vacation season.

2 *Listen to the excerpt again. Choose the correct answer.*

B _____

Listen to each sentence. Circle the meaning of the words you hear.

1. Cherokees believe it is wrong to unnecessarily <u>take the life</u> of an animal.
2. My neighbor uses a noisy leaf blower to <u>gather</u> the leaves in his yard.
3. Making one quick start with the car may not use that much more gasoline. It's the <u>sum</u> of doing it all the time that leads to wasted gas.
4. On religious holidays, people like to go to <u>sacred</u> places to worship and pray.
5. They don't have a dishwasher, a sewing machine, or a washing machine. They prefer to do those things <u>manually</u>.

C _____

Listen to the excerpts. Circle the word that best completes each sentence.

1. He always has to win! He does everything so . . .
2. I'm trying to recycle rather than throw away things I don't use. I'm trying not to be so . . .
3. Pollution increases the more a country becomes . . .
4. You can't hunt the bald eagle in the United States. It's . . .
5. Don't throw that can in the trash! You should . . .

D _____

Listen to the words. Circle the word you hear.

1. zinc
2. sought
3. tread
4. those
5. path

E _____

Listen to each dialogue. Circle the sentence that best sums up each conversation.

1. A: Rom, did you throw out the bottles I was collecting?
   B: Yeah, why?
   A: There was a ten-cent deposit on each. You could've taken them to the recycling center and gotten a refund.
   B: Oh, sorry Ellen, I didn't know that. I'll hang on to them next time.

2. A: There's a big oil spot on the ground over on the side of the house. Were you changing the oil in your car there, Mick?
   B: Yeah. Sorry about the mess.
   A: Next time please put a pan down to catch the oil. It's not just the mess; it's bad for the environment.
   B: Yeah, I'm sorry about that. I promise I'll do it next time.

3. A: You know, Kizza, these milk cartons are recyclable.
   B: What do you do with them?
   A: I just rinse them and flatten them. When they're dry, I throw them in this box under the sink.
   B: That's a good system, Kazumi. I'll put them in there from now on.

4. A: Oh, Toti really did a good job raking up the leaves.
   B: He sure did; the yard looks really nice. . . . Uh-oh, what's that? Did he burn the leaves?
   A: No, I'm sure he didn't. He knows not to do that.
   B: Yeah, he's never burned the leaves. It must have been the neighbor's kids, I guess.

5. A: I wish I had that old lumber that I threw out!
   B: What do you need it for, Alan?
   A: I'm building some shelves in the stock room and that wood would've been perfect.
   B: Oh, that's too bad.

F _____

Listen to each dialogue. Circle the word or phrase that best completes each sentence.

1. **Dave:** Eric, you can't throw out glass with burnable garbage.
   Eric: Oh, sorry. I'll take it out.

2. **Amanda:** Rex, don't throw away your old newspapers. The local school is collecting old papers in a drive to raise money.
   Rex: But they can't use these. There's paint all over them.

3. **Nicole:** What do you think of my new hybrid car, Elizabeth?
   Elizabeth: It's great, Nicole!

UNIT 6

A _____

1 *Listen to the excerpt. Mark each sentence **T** (true) or **F** (false).*

Approximately 72 percent of Americans donate to charity, and 51 percent do volunteer work. About 2 million not-for-profit organizations and charities in the United States today receive this help.

There are three types of philanthropists: individual, foundations, and private corporations. Individuals give money or volunteer their time to support causes that are important to them. Foundations are organizations started by very wealthy individuals. Their "business" is not to make a profit but to give money away to not-for-profits. Private corporations may also use a portion of their business profits to make donations, or they may give away their products or services free of charge. However, foundations and corporations are responsible for only 20 percent of charitable donations; 80 percent comes from individuals.

What makes people and institutions give away their time and money? One reason is altruism, the unselfish desire to help other people and make the world a better place. Other reasons involve personal interest. Under U.S. tax law, an individual or business does not have to pay income tax on money that is donated to charity. For extremely wealthy individuals and corporations, this can mean millions of dollars they do not have to pay to the government. In addition to tax benefits, donors (people and companies who give) often receive favorable publicity for making donations, and they have an opportunity to influence the world around them.

2 *Listen to the excerpt again. Circle the word or phrase that best completes each sentence.*

B

Listen to the sentences and key words. Circle the meaning of the words you hear.

1. I know several people who belong to Caritas, a church-based <u>charity</u>.
2. Luis <u>donates</u> to political organizations, but he never talks about politics.
3. <u>Philanthropists</u> come from different backgrounds and have different reasons for what they do.
4. Before the university can approve any <u>scholarship</u>, the board of directors has to decide how it should be awarded.
5. Any <u>recipient</u> of a donation from the foundation must use it only for farm research.
6. Vladimir was <u>stunned</u> when he discovered the identity of his benefactor.
7. Is a <u>benefactor</u> required to report his donation on his income tax return?
8. Mark and Yasmina are deciding whether they should touch their <u>nest egg</u> and start a used-clothes shop now.
9. "I <u>pledge</u> $5,000 worth of new books for the library," Eric announced at his high school reunion.
10. Elsa is hoping that her parents will <u>fund</u> her volunteer work in India.

C

*Listen to the tag questions, and draw intonation lines. Mark each sentence **C** (comment) or **Q** (question) according to the intonation.*

_____ 1. Gladys Holm's $18 million donation will be used to fund heart disease research, won't it?

_____ 2. Bill Gates really cares about the world's poor children, doesn't he?

_____ 3. You must be at least 21 years old to be a fire brigade volunteer, mustn't you?

_____ 4. If your father were alive today, he'd be proud to see you helping people build houses, wouldn't he?

_____ 5. Philanthropists shouldn't always expect to be thanked for their efforts, should they?

_____ 6. Dress for Success doesn't only provide free clothing, does it?

D

Complete each sentence with a tag question.

1. Mrs. Swanson has been donating books to the school library, . . . ?
2. Rebecca was a volunteer for Doctors Without Borders, . . . ?
3. The university can't offer any more scholarships, . . . ?
4. You haven't touched our nest egg, . . . ?
5. Village residents couldn't organize a citizen's watch, . . . ?
6. Kai convinced his boss to pledge 50 hours of computer service to the community center, . . . ?

UNIT 7

A

1 *Listen to the excerpt. Mark each sentence **T** (true) or **F** (false).*

Since their development, intelligence tests have been widely used in U.S. schools to evaluate students' abilities and predict their success. However, they have also been criticized for several reasons.

IQ tests do not accurately predict a person's success in life. This criticism has been supported by research. One study followed 450 boys who were given IQ tests. Researchers found that an IQ score did not predict whether a boy would have a happy, productive life. They found that 7 percent of men with an IQ under 80 (below average intelligence) were unemployed for much of the time. But they also found that 7 percent of men with an IQ over 100 (above average intelligence) were unemployed. Clearly, these men needed more than intelligence, as defined by the IQ test, to have successful careers.

Recent theories of intelligence include emotional intelligence, or EQ. According to American psychologist Daniel Goleman, emotional intelligence includes skills such as understanding one's own emotions and relating well to other people.

2 Listen to the excerpt again. Circle the correct sentence in each pair.

B _____

Listen to each dialogue. Circle the sentence that best sums up each conversation.

1. **A:** My dinner's cold, Barb. I think I'll send it back.
   B: Oh, Nat, please don't make a fuss.

2. **A:** Grandpa never seems to throw anything away, does he, Mom?
   B: Well, try to empathize with him, Jane. People didn't waste things when times were hard.

3. **A:** Man! I can't believe I sprained my ankle. I'll miss the big game next week.
   B: I know it's a setback, Eric . . . but in a couple of weeks, you'll be out there again.
   A: Yeah, I guess I shouldn't dwell on it. Thanks, Ken.

4. **A:** Can you believe it? Kay was promoted to manager and I wasn't!
   B: Yes, it doesn't seem fair, Jan. No one deserves a promotion more than you do.
   A: But now I just need to put aside any negative feelings so we can work productively together.
   B: Yeah, you can't be resentful because she got the promotion.

5. **A:** [whistles]
   B: You're always so cheerful on the job, Mary Ann.
   A: I try to be, Laurie. I think it's important to have an enthusiastic outlook on life.

6. **A:** Gwen sure does a lot of non–work related activity during office hours: reading magazines, sending personal e-mail . . .
   B: Yes, and I suggested to her that she should use her time more productively, but she didn't respond well to my advice.

7. **A:** Nothing seems to fluster Don. Even when things get busy around here.
   B: Yeah, he just keeps working. He's steady and always pleasant to be around.
   A: He just sort of takes life in stride.

8. **A:** Poor Francis. He got all the answers wrong on the quiz.
   B: Yeah . . . I wanted to study with him, but he insisted that he didn't need to study.
   A: It's difficult for him to swallow his pride.

C _____

Listen to the words. Put a dot over the syllable with the strongest stress. Write a schwa [ə] over the vowels that are pronounced "uh."

1. intelligence   5. empathy
2. enthusiasm   6. allowances
3. negative   7. positive
4. unemployed

D _____

Listen to each statement. Circle the sentence that expresses the statement in indirect speech.

1. My IQ is 140.
2. I may need to stay late at work this evening.
3. Marty's going to the hockey game on Saturday.
4. You must take the IQ test.
5. Nicki studied psychology in college.
6. I must take the IQ test tomorrow.
7. Have you ever taken an EQ test?
8. Mensa welcomes people whose IQ is in the top 2 percent of the population.

UNIT 8

A _____

1 Listen to the telephone conversations. Complete each sentence with the correct name.

Julie: Hello?

Stephen: Hi, Julie? It's Stephen. I'm sorry to call you up before the math test, but you said you wanted to try that new sandwich place you read about—*Au Pain Gourmet*.

Julie: Oh, I read about it in the paper. Apparently people are lining up around the block to give it a try.

Stephen: Yeah, I'd like to check it out, too. . . . Why don't you come over tomorrow morning? We can finish our homework, and then, we can go out for a walk and get one of those baguette sandwiches.

Julie: Stephen, I don't know . . . See . . . Bill was talking about getting together.

Stephen: What was that? Oh, your friend Bill? Well, can't you turn him down? Just put it off until another time.

Julie: Well, I . . . I'll try. OK.

Stephen: OK. Bye.

(an hour or two later)

Bill: Hello?

Julie: Hi, Bill. This is Julie. How are you?

Bill: Hey, Julie! How are you? I'm looking forward to—

Julie: Bill, hold on a minute. . . . Listen, I know you offered to cook lunch for me tomorrow, but I'm afraid I have to cancel.

Bill: What do you mean, call it off?

Julie: Yes, I know I'm letting you down, but I was thinking it over and I don't know if I can spare the time. I'm working on a big math project for school, and we have to hand it in on Monday. Maybe some other time?

Bill: But, Julie! Well, OK. I'll just wait until you're available since you're the only girl I want to date.

Julie: Bill, I'm sorry. I was hoping I could work it out, but I . . . What's that noise?

Bill: Oops, hang on a minute. I have another call. Could you hold for a minute?

Julie: Well, actually, can you call me back later?

Bill: I can't, but we'll see each other around. I'll talk to you soon, OK?

Julie: OK, bye.

2 *Listen to the conversations again. Mark each sentence* ***T*** *(true) or* ***F*** *(false).*

B _____

Listen to the sentences and key words. Circle the meaning of the words you hear.

1. I really don't know where I'll get the <u>dough</u> to buy all those delicacies that my friends want me to bring back from Thailand.
2. For some time now, there's been <u>trouble brewing</u> between the chef and his assistant and everyone's afraid that one of these days, things will explode.
3. Is it true that the demand for tofu became so great that it <u>stirred up</u> fierce competition among tofu shops?
4. The feminization of the workplace gave Marco some <u>food for thought</u> when he was creating his restaurant's new menu.
5. The fact that Lucia is now the sole <u>breadwinner</u> is hard for Gerard to swallow.
6. The health ministry is overrun with consultants. In one year, no project has ever been finished. <u>Too many cooks spoil the broth</u>.
7. Her chocolate cake was such a hit with family and friends that she started her own pastry business. Now other people do the cooking for her while she <u>brings home the bacon</u>.
8. Hector secretly prefers take-out fast food to Rossini's dinner creations, but he encourages her to <u>let her imagination run wild</u> in the kitchen and praises her cooking highly.
9. Although Darlene sometimes organizes wedding receptions, catering for small parties and intimate gatherings is really her <u>bread and butter</u>.
10. Beverage companies are <u>shifting</u> to healthier drinks that appeal to diet-conscious consumers.

C _____

Listen to the words. Pay attention to the sound of the underlined letters.

S<u>o</u>me	H<u>o</u>t
G<u>oo</u>d	F<u>oo</u>d
C<u>o</u>ld	

Now listen to these words. Circle the symbol with the same sound as the underlined letters.

1. <u>o</u>nion
2. c<u>oo</u>kie
3. y<u>o</u>gurt
4. p<u>o</u>t
5. n<u>oo</u>dles

D _____

Listen to the conversations. Write the phrasal verb from the list below that best completes each conversation.

1. **A:** Hey, Stella. We need to invite one more guy to the dinner party.
   B: I'll call Charlie and _____.
2. **A:** You know, I've never tasted Thai food. Maybe I should experiment a little. What do you think?
   B: I bet you'd like it. You should _____.
3. **A:** Has the caterer returned my phone call yet?
   B: I don't think so. Did he say that he'll _____?
4. **A:** Guess who I met on the way to the restroom?
   B: A movie star?
   A: Are you kidding? This restaurant is so bad, a movie star is the last person that we could _____.
5. **A:** I've considered your partnership offer and I'll accept it.
   B: Great! You're the best chef we've ever had and I'm so glad you didn't _____.
6. **A:** Did you ever get around to canning those beans or did you decide to postpone that until next weekend?
   B: Maybe I'll do it next weekend. Just thinking about it tired me out so I decided to _____.
7. **A:** Will you look at that rain? Do you think they'll cancel the picnic?
   B: What? And break a century-old company tradition? No, there is no way they will _____.
8. **A:** Wait! Don't start the mixer until you've put all the ingredients together in the bowl.
   B: Oops! I should have waited for you to tell me when to _____.

UNIT 9

A _____

1 *Listen to the excerpt. Mark each sentence* ***T*** *(true) or* ***F*** *(false).*

In his home country of Mexico, Esteban was an active, outgoing young man. He was optimistic, full of life, and had many friends. Esteban was also an excellent student.

When he was 16, his father was transferred to the United States, and the family moved with him. This was a very difficult adjustment for Esteban, who felt uprooted from his home. At school, the American kids were friendly to him, but he couldn't seem to blend in. Instead of feeling excited by his new classes, he felt intimidated. His teachers tried to encourage him. They suggested that he join clubs in order to meet other students. Esteban appreciated their support, but his feeling of being a foreigner set him apart from the others. Sometimes he had difficulty communicating with his classmates, and there was no one who spoke his language who could interpret for him. He felt that no one would ever listen to him or value his opinion.

His unhappiness extended to his family life, too. Although Esteban's family was very tight-knit, he did not want to talk to them about his problems. Instead, he suppressed his sad feelings so his parents wouldn't worry about him. He thought that if only he knew more English, he would be able to make friends more easily and feel more comfortable. Esteban's frustration grew. Eventually, he felt unable to deal with even the smallest day-to-day tasks. Sometimes he disliked the United States and English and felt that he would never adjust.

2 *Listen to the excerpt again. Circle the correct answer.*

B

Listen to the statements and read the corresponding sentences below. Circle whether the meaning is the same or different from the statements you hear.

1. Emma's native tongue is German.
2. Frank comes from a tight-knit family.
3. Jon plans to bone up for his Japanese test this weekend.
4. Yoshino was relieved to get her visa.
5. Speaking a new language to a native speaker is often intimidating.
6. Ken's language skills are unique among his classmates.
7. Immigrant communities will continue to flourish in the United States.
8. Many immigrants want to be part of mainstream life in their new countries.

C

Listen to the words. Pay attention to the sound of the underlined letters.

Immigra<u>ti</u>on	Cul<u>t</u>ure
Deci<u>si</u>on	Language

Now listen to these words. Circle the symbol with the same sound as the underlined letters.

1. na<u>t</u>ural
2. exten<u>si</u>on
3. refugee
4. A<u>si</u>a
5. deporta<u>ti</u>on
6. Cauca<u>si</u>an

D

*Listen to the sentences. Circle **same** if the statement uses only one verb tense. Circle **contrasting** if the statement uses more than one verb tense.*

1. On the first day of school, Dr. Chin's mother didn't understand what the teacher was talking about.
2. Today, Dr. Chin's mother doesn't speak Chinese very well, and she can't read or write it.
3. Dr. Chin's mother hasn't spoken Chinese since she was a little girl, so she doesn't remember how to speak it any more.
4. Our world is getting smaller and smaller as communication technology improves.
5. More people are traveling to foreign countries and choosing to live there.
6. According to Dr. Chin, people's attitudes have changed a lot since she was a young girl.
7. She sees this change of attitude whenever she looks at her own children.
8. Dr. Chin's children are Chinese Americans who are learning to speak Chinese for the first time.

UNIT 10

A

1 *Listen to the excerpt. Circle the sentence that best expresses each main idea.*

Steve Curwood: Modern life is full of nasty noises, especially in the cities. Sirens can shatter serenity at any moment, and jackhammers, loud music, and useless mufflers can all send us over the edge. For many people in New York City, there's one form of sonic pollution at the top of the list. They're calling for its banning, even though some nervous New Yorkers savor the sound for security reasons. And as Neal Rauch reports, even as the controversy prompts loud debate, some aren't waiting for laws to be passed.

Neal Rauch: A music producer and composer, this resident of Manhattan's Upper West Side got fed up with car alarms disturbing his sleep and his work. He got together with some similarly frazzled neighbors and formed a posse of sorts.

Man: We start out with a note saying, "Fix your car alarm. It disturbed hundreds of people last night." If that doesn't help we quite often use some minor retaliatory step like breaking an egg on their windshield or on the front hood, which doesn't hurt anything but it's a little bit of a mess to clean up. . . . Another classic is to smear Vaseline all over the windshield, which is incredibly hard to get off. So . . . I think in other neighborhoods there might be even broken windshields and things like that.

Catherine Abate: The noise affects not only their ability to sleep at night, but for the most part their ability to work during the day. And even parents have come to me and said, "What is the impact on children?" And there are more and more studies that show that young people in particular, that are exposed to a sustained amount of loud noise, have hearing loss. So it's a health issue; it's a quality of life issue.

Neil Rauch: Enforcement of existing laws, along with new regulations, may be cutting down noise in some neighborhoods. It's now illegal for alarms to run for more than three minutes. After that, police can break into a car and disable the alarm or even tow away a wailing vehicle. It's hoped these actions will motivate car owners to adjust their alarms, making them less sensitive so vibrations from passing trucks and the like don't set them off.

2 *Listen to the excerpt again. Circle the fact that is not in the excerpt.*

B _____

Listen to each sentence. Circle the meaning of the word or phrase you hear.

1. The Yoders moved to the country, thinking nothing would <u>shatter</u> their peace and quiet, until the government decided to build a highway outside their doorstep.
2. "If our neighbors don't stop banging their doors," Joseph's grandmother declared, "it'll <u>send me over the edge</u>!"
3. Put your clock under your pillow so that when it <u>goes off</u>, it won't disturb your roommate.
4. This building is so old that we feel <u>vibrations</u> every time a truck rolls by.
5. When the kerosene supply reaches a certain level, it <u>prompts</u> the heater to beep.
6. The sound of screeching tires <u>jolted</u> Sandra out of her sleep.

7. Can they <u>tow away</u> my car just because I have the stereo on too loud?
8. Ever since the road construction crew started working outside her window, Tala has had a <u>nagging</u> headache.
9. The city government has <u>banned</u> motorcycles without mufflers from the streets.
10. The anti-noise <u>vigilantes</u> are becoming more aggressive every day.

C _____

Listen to the excerpt. Circle the particles that are stressed.

I think they're bullies. They walk <u>around</u> in a group and show <u>off</u> by destroying other people's property. They think they can just act <u>up</u> and no one will fight <u>back</u>. Well, I'm fed <u>up</u>. I'm taking them to court.

D _____

Listen to the sentences. Circle the verb tense used in each sentence.

1. According to the doctor, by the end of this year, Clarissa will have lost 50 percent of her hearing in her right ear.
2. Will you be using these headphones for the television later tonight?
3. Cars in the next decade will be faster, safer, and quieter.
4. In two years, Gene will have finished his project on sonic pollution and its effects on fish.
5. Nico will join the vigilantes that punish noisemakers in his neighborhood.
6. By morning, Amram's car will have been towed away by the neighborhood posse.
7. Malik won't be removing his car alarm tomorrow or any other day after that.
8. By tomorrow evening, the community will have voted on the measure against the loud stereo shop.

Achievement Tests
Test 1 Answer Key

UNIT 1

A

☐1 1. F   2. T   3. F

☐2 1. history
2. medieval
3. has
4. Mommy's

B

1. b   6. c
2. c   7. b
3. a   8. c
4. c   9. c
5. a   10. a

C

1. has   4. have
2. 've   5. are
3. 's

D

1. present progressive
2. past
3. present perfect
4. present
5. past
6. past perfect
7. base form
8. future

UNIT 2

A

☐1 1. F   2. T   3. T   4. T

☐2 1. lips
2. angry
3. an incubator
4. Braille

B

1. a   6. a
2. b   7. b
3. a   8. a
4. a   9. a
5. b   10. b

C

1. b   2. a   3. a   4. b

D

1. It was Leila's first time using crutches /
   and she had a difficult time turning around.
2. Sales of the new wheelchair have been so strong /
   that the company is turning around /
   and is number one in sales again.
3. It's difficult for my grandmother, /
   who has arthritis, /
   to reach deep down into the washing machine /
   to remove clothes.
4. If you want to accomplish great deeds, /
   you have to reach deep down into yourself /
   and bring out the best in yourself.

E

1. to know   3. walking
2. to enter   4. installing

UNIT 3

A

☐1 1. a   2. a   3. a   4. b
☐2 1. T   2. F   3. T   4. T

B

1. c   6. c
2. b   7. b
3. a   8. a
4. b   9. b
5. a   10. c

C

1. eyes, looking; mind, else
2. sleep, little; wake, lot
3. Joshua, all the time; wife, never
4. common; serious
5. surges, energy, night; waves, sleepiness, day

D

1. you would feel less sleepy.
2. she might have more time for her children.
3. they would be more alert during operations.
4. teenagers might be more attentive in school.
5. I could sleep better at night.
6. he could get to work before his manager.
7. she would have been promoted.

UNIT 4

A _____

1 1. F 2. T 3. F 4. T

2 1. waves 3. shock
2. porches 4. blew up

B _____

1. a 6. a
2. c 7. a
3. b 8. b
4. c 9. c
5. c 10. c

C _____

1. b 2. b 3. a 4. b

D _____

1. In his lifetime, Miguel has experienced hurricanes, floods, landslides, forest fires, and droughts.

2. The different parts of a hurricane are: the eye of the storm, the eye wall, and the hurricane's tail.

3. By the time the forest fire was put out, 181 people were dead, 253 were injured, 8,500 were left homeless, and $150 million worth of property was destroyed.

4. We have no electricity, no water, no food, and no warm clothes.

E _____

1. b 2. a 3. b 4. a

UNIT 5

A _____

1 1. a 2. b 3. a
2 1. b 2. a 3. b 4. a

B _____

1. b 2. a 3. c 4. b 5. c

C _____

1. c 2. b 3. c 4. c 5. b

D _____

1. c 2. a 3. c 4. b 5. c

E _____

1. a 2. b 3. a 4. a 5. a

F _____

1. a 2. c 3. a

UNIT 6

A _____

1 1. F 2. F 3. T 4. T
2 1. b 2. c 3. b 4. a

B _____

1. a 6. a
2. b 7. b
3. b 8. a
4. b 9. b
5. a 10. b

C _____

1. Q, rising intonation
2. C, falling intonation
3. Q, rising intonation
4. C, falling intonation
5. C, falling intonation
6. Q, rising intonation

D _____

1. hasn't she?
2. wasn't she?
3. can it?
4. have you?
5. could they?
6. didn't he?

UNIT 7

A _____

1 1. T 2. F 3. F
2 1. b 2. b 3. a 4. a

B _____

1. a 5. a
2. b 6. b
3. a 7. a
4. a 8. a

C _____

1. in•tel•li•gence
2. en•thu•si•asm
3. ne•ga•tive
4. un•em•ployed
5. em•pa•thy
6. al•low•an•ces
7. po•si•tive

D _____

1. b	5. b
2. a	6. a
3. b	7. b
4. b	8. a

UNIT 8

A _____

1. 1. Stephen
2. Bill
3. Julie
2. 1. T   2. T   3. T   4. F

B _____

1. b	6. c
2. a	7. b
3. a	8. a
4. b	9. a
5. c	10. c

C _____

1. b   2. b   3. a   4. a   5. b

D _____

1. ask him over	5. turn it down
2. try it out	6. put it off
3. call back	7. call it off
4. run into	8. turn it on

UNIT 9

A _____

1. 1. T   2. F   3. T   4. T
2. 1. b   2. c   3. a   4. c

B _____

1. same	5. different
2. same	6. same
3. same	7. same
4. same	8. different

C _____

1. a	4. b
2. a	5. a
3. a	6. b

D _____

1. b	5. a
2. a	6. b
3. b	7. a
4. b	8. b

UNIT 10

A _____

1. 1. b   2. a   3. b   4. b
2. 1. c   2. a   3. b

B _____

1. a	6. c
2. c	7. b
3. b	8. a
4. b	9. b
5. a	10. a

C _____

1. around
2. off
3. up
4. back
5. up

D _____

1. b	5. a
2. c	6. b
3. a	7. c
4. b	8. b

Notes

TEST 1
1. Audio Program Introduction

UNIT 1
2. A. 1
3. Excerpt *(for A1 and A2)*
4. A. 2
5. B.
6. C.
7. D.

UNIT 2
8. A. 1
9. Excerpt *(for A1 and A2)*
10. A. 2
11. B.
12. C.
13. D.
14. E.

UNIT 3
15. A. 1
16. Excerpt *(for A1 and A2)*
17. A. 2
18. B.
19. C.
20. D.

UNIT 4
21. A. 1
22. Excerpt *(for A1 and A2)*
23. A. 2
24. B.
25. C.
26. D.
27. E.

UNIT 5
28. A. 1
29. Excerpt *(for A1 and A2)*
30. A. 2
31. B.
32. C.
33. D.
34. E.
35. F.

UNIT 6
36. A. 1
37. Excerpt *(for A1 and A2)*
38. A. 2
39. B.
40. C.
41. D.

UNIT 7
42. A. 1
43. Excerpt *(for A1 and A2)*
44. A. 2
45. B.
46. C.
47. D.

UNIT 8
48. A. 1
49. Conversations *(for A1 and A2)*
50. A. 2
51. B.
52. C.
53. D.

UNIT 9
54. A. 1
55. Conversations *(for A1 and A2)*
56. A. 2
57. B.
58. C.
59. D.

UNIT 10
60. A. 1
61. Excerpt *(for A1 and A2)*
62. A. 2
63. B.
64. C.
65. D.